This Journal Belongs to

....

Published by Barbour Publishing, Inc., 1810 Barbour Drive, Uhrichsville, Ohio 44683, www.barbourbooks.com.

Our mission is to inspire the world with the life-changing message of the Bible.

Member of the
Evangelical Christian
Publishers Association

Printed in China.

Marian Leslie

Untroubled

A Devotional Journal
for Finding Calm in a Chaotic World

BARBOUR
PUBLISHING

To Maggie,
because this is what
I want your heart to be.

Introduction

"I have told you these things, so that in me you may have peace. In this world you will have trouble. But take heart! I have overcome the world."

JOHN 16:33

Carefree. Laid-back. Easygoing. Happy-go-lucky. Do you relate to these descriptions at all?

These days, who does? With so many troubles, how could we ever hope to escape them? Can we really even imagine a world without worries?

Probably not. But being untroubled doesn't mean you won't experience problems. You will. Jesus said so. In this world, in this crazy, hectic, worn-out, mixed-up, weary world, you will have trouble. You will know hard days. You will know whole terrible months. You will trudge through grief and slog through disappointment and trek through trials. You may even feel so bad, you will want to give up.

Jesus knew about that kind of sorrow and disappointment and affliction. He knew, because He walked on this earth, through the dust and the mud and the heat and the rain. He knew what it was to have a bad day. He knew what it was to experience great pain—both heart-heavy aches and flesh-searing anguish.

And yet He promised, "I have overcome the world."

Being untroubled doesn't mean you'll have no shadows on your path. It just means Jesus will be by your side, lighting the way. Jesus is the great Untroubler—unraveling the knots of your anxiety and bringing peace to your panic.

Let's follow in the footsteps of the Prince of Peace and "take heart" as we reflect on His Word together.

With Every Breath

Let everything that has breath praise the LORD.
PSALM 150:6

In. Out. In. Out. In. . . Breathing isn't something most of us have to think about. It's not hard to do. It is our body's involuntary response to the air.

But for some, breathing is a struggle. For the asthmatic and those afflicted with certain disorders or diseases, breathing can feel like a battle between your will and your windpipe. Panic rises as a person fights for every molecule of oxygen. Fear fills the mind as the lungs attempt to fill with air. One episode like this can steal a person's energy for an entire day.

Even those of us who are not suffering from any chronic breathing troubles have probably at some time felt out of breath. After strenuous exercise, we may have bent over, huffing and puffing as we tried to regain the normal rhythm of in and out, in and out. Or in a moment of fright, we may have sucked in air rapidly in a gasp and felt our heartbeat speed up. Maybe on a first date with a special someone, we have become acutely aware of the breathing process, reminding ourselves to keep on doing it. . .in and out, in and out. Or during a time of grief, when our body ached with sorrow, we may have sobbed and gulped in great mouthfuls of air that only seemed to add to the heaviness of our thoughts.

Psalm 150 is a song of praise to God. Every line, one after another, offers praise. Next time you are feeling anxious, try breathing this praise to God in and out. As we praise Him, we can remember why He is worthy to be praised. We praise Him because of who He is, the God of peace in His sanctuary, the God of power in the mighty heavens. And because He is who He is, and because He has given us everything, and because He is in control of every-thing, we can praise Him with everything—with the sounds of our lives that are soft and calm, like the lullabies we sing over babies, or the breaths of sleeping children. We can praise Him with sounds of celebration, and we can praise Him with our loudness—even in our shouts of surprise, or anger, or sorrow. In all the sounds of our human emotions, we can praise the God who gives us every breath—the God who is with us even before we take in air at birth for our first breath, and the God who waits for us as we exhale our last.

Lord of every breath in and every breath out,
I thank You for breathing Your Spirit into me. Amen.

Fanciful Works

How countless are your works, LORD! In wisdom you
have made them all; the earth is full of your creatures.
PSALM 104:24 CSB

Flitting, fluttering, flying by. They look so delicate and beautiful, like bits of stained glass that have somehow gotten loose and been carried away on the wind. They fly this way and that, seeming to have no pattern or purpose. They have no worries or cares. They do not mind the headlines. They are the picture of frivolity—colorful bits of wonder dancing on the flowers.

But butterflies are not the magical, whimsical fairies we make them out to be. They are hard workers. They are busy. They are gathering fuel. They are travelers. They have places to go and things to do. Their lives are relatively short, and they must prepare for the next generation.

There is beauty and grace in their tasks. Beauty and grace in the way they move and the colors they display. They do not make the colors—they are painted by the hand of God, designed by Him, no doubt for His pleasure, and placed here for us to enjoy as well. And yet we see in the butterfly diligence and perseverance too. Pushing those fragile wings against the elements is hard work. Thousands of tiny chitin scales create their elegant armor, allow them to absorb heat, and filter the wind in just the right way to let them lift off and flutter away.

Beauty and grace and hard work are built into all of God's creation. Read Psalm 104 and you will see it in each line. Light spreading out like a canopy over a palace of water and wind, earth and fire. Mountains rising majestic and valleys sinking with the weight of green provision. "The earth is satisfied by the fruit of your labor," the psalmist writes to God (verse 13 CSB). We are the beneficiaries of the Lord's diligence and perseverance, of His perfect attention and care. He created things to grow and sustain, but more than that, to delight and thrive.

As we look at the beauty of nature all around us, fluttering by in glimpses of glory, let us admire and be inspired, not just by the color and light, but by the complexity and thought and painstaking labor of our tireless Master, who knows all and provides everything we need, and more than we can ever imagine. And let us work to reflect His excellence in everything we do.

Lord of all works beautiful and amazing, and all things sound and supporting,
I praise You today. I thank You for a world in which I can rest and
be refreshed, and work to bring You glory. Amen.

The Danger of Strangers

So now you Gentiles are no longer strangers and foreigners. You are citizens along with all of God's holy people. You are members of God's family.
EPHESIANS 2:19 NLT

Strangers. When we are children, we are taught to be on guard around them—to not speak to them. "Stranger danger." Fear and mistrust are built into us even before we learn these lessons—what is often termed "separation anxiety." It's that feeling of momentary panic that comes over children upon being made to leave their parents' arms. What must go through their little minds? To have their arms unwrapped from the neck they know, the one that smells of safety and home and sustenance, and to be held instead by a different body with a strange scent and an unfamiliar voice. It's no wonder they cry out and complain and protest. They cannot understand that the leaving is for just a little while and that soon their loved one will be restored to them. They have a hard time switching off the inborn need for their family and recognizing the fun to be had in the new world they have been thrust into.

We sometimes seem to have the opposite problem. We have fallen in love with the fun of our new world and forgotten the need for our family—for the family of God. We crave the land of pleasure, the company of strangers, and forget the safety and solidity of the One who first loved us and breathed life into us.

But as Paul told the believers of the church in Ephesus, we are no longer people living in a foreign land, ignorant of the Church's beliefs and standards and history. We are no longer outsiders looking in. We are no longer the strangers we had learned to be. We are instead members of the kingdom of God. We are God's. We belong to Him. We can wrap our arms tightly around His neck and breathe in the aroma of His holiness and know we are home. We are safe. We are loved.

Our lives here are temporary. We should not get so familiar with our experiences in this land that we forget who we are. We should instead cling to God's promises, learn His language of love and mercy, and remember the history He has lived with His people. We should spend time with Him and let Him take care of us. We should read His Word and hear what He wants for us and what He demands of us. We can find peace in His arms, healing in His hands, calm in His thoughts.

God, my Father, remind me that I am Yours. Amen.

Let the Rejoicing Begin

"I tell you that in the same way there will be more rejoicing in heaven over one sinner who repents than over ninety-nine righteous persons who do not need to repent."
LUKE 15:7

. . . .

What was it this week? Did you lie about where you had to be so you could get out of an awkward experience? Did you skimp on your work hours? Did you have angry, hateful thoughts about that neighbor who always, always lets his dog fertilize your yard? Did you spew hurtful words against a family member? Did you cheat? Did you steal? Did you. . .

Chances are, there's been more than one time this week when you felt like you messed up. Big-time. And maybe you really did do something wrong deliberately. Maybe you didn't. Either way, the feelings of guilt and regret and shame pile up. They color everything you do and every thought you have about yourself. After a while, they keep you from even knowing where to begin to do better.

But beginning means ending. It means stopping what we have been doing and saying and thinking, and taking one moment, one breath to turn away and say, "God, I'm sorry. I need help." This is the start of the unraveling of trouble. This is where we unwind ourselves from the tangle of temptations and emotions and sins that strangle, and begin to fill our lungs with words of truth. This is where we bend our wills to the one will of God. This is where we surrender. This is where we lay ourselves down and take up His cross.

And when we do that, the rejoicing begins. You may wonder, *Why such a party for just one who repents?* But the party is not just for the one. It's for the One. Because when one turns around and is forgiven, beautiful things happen, rippling out from that one freed heart. They are brought one step away from death and begin the path of life. They are saved from more moments of suffering. They escape the trap of the devil (2 Timothy 2:26). They open their minds to more truth, more love, more wisdom, more peace. More life. They can look forward to "times of refreshing" (Acts 3:19). Whole nations can be saved when just one begins the wave of repentance. Redemption and restoration come to those who repent. And God receives the glory.

Lord God, my part in Your kingdom sometimes seems so small, yet I know the weight of my sins is enough to tear others down. I repent today of what I have done and thought, and I ask You to restore me. Let the rejoicing begin today. Amen.

Mourning

When my prayers returned to me unanswered,
I went about mourning as though for my friend or brother.
PSALM 35:13–14

When someone we love dies, grief is understandable. People have compassion for us. Feeling sad about the loss of a special person in our lives is, unfortunately, a familiar occurrence for us all.

But there are other kinds and causes of grief. And some of those are harder for people to identify and comprehend and evaluate.

If you've ever been ridiculed, bullied, humiliated, or embarrassed, you may know this grief. If you've ever had people rejoice in your blunders or be glad for your failings, you may understand this kind of sorrow.

What are we grieving in times like these? We are mourning the love we could be experiencing. We are mourning the friends we wish we could count. We are mourning the absence of the person we want to be.

And that is hard. Sometimes it might even be harder than mourning a death.

This kind of grief sticks around for a while. Its scars are hard to shake. We hear the echoes of insults in our mind and we start to think those words sound like truth. This kind of grief can cause damaging wounds that stay raw and sting for years and years, affecting our relationships, our self-image, and our walk with God.

David knew this grief. He knew what it was like to be laughed at. He knew what it was like to have people out to get him. He knew what it was like to be hated and fought against. He described his foes as lions, gnashing their teeth, waiting for the moment they could bring him down. And he pleaded with God, "You have seen this; do not be silent. Do not be far from me, Lord" (Psalm 35:22).

David knew where he could go for help. He knew God would see his grief and understand it. He knew God was never far from him but rather was as close as a heartbeat. He knew he could trust God to protect him from the pain, heal his wounds, and save his life from ruin. We can too. And like David, we can say, "My tongue will proclaim your righteousness, your praises all day long" (verse 28).

God, sometimes I feel as if the whole world is out to get me, even when there might be only a few voices speaking against me. Help me to see the truth. And help me to trust that You understand me and will always, always be there for me. Amen.

Wounds Bound

He heals the brokenhearted and binds up their wounds.
PSALM 147:3

Heaviness. Depression. Sorrow. Loss of appetite. Numbness. Anger. These are all perfectly normal reactions to losing someone you love. And while so many of us experience these same reactions to loss, there is something about grief that tricks us into believing we are walking all alone.

But we are never alone. Not even for one gasping, sobbing breath.

Anyone who is grieving can find an understanding friend in the psalmists. In Psalms we find someone who knows what it feels like to consume sorrow: "My tears have been my food day and night" (42:3). We hear the familiar self-doubting questions and the whispers of encouragement we speak to ourselves in response, desperate to cling to some cobweb of hope and praying the stickiness will be enough to hang on to our souls and keep us from falling completely away: "Why, my soul, are you downcast? Why so disturbed within me? Put your hope in God, for I will yet praise him, my Savior and my God" (verse 11).

The psalms remind us not only that other humans understand the weight of our grief, but that even more, one great and mighty God cares about every question we want to ask, every angry rage we fly into, and every tear that races down our wet cheeks. And it is this God who rounds us up from our self-imposed exile in the country of despair and gathers us into His arms. It is this God, the One who knows us intimately—as He knows the name of every star. It is this God who has the power to stretch out space and powder it with planets, who has understanding enough to reach into the farthest parts of our gloomy hearts. It is this God who provides sustenance for every living creature who also knows how to feed our hope and make joy grow again.

This God not only takes delight in those who are strong and can keep on marching into battle; He smiles into the faces of those who are filled with fear and weak with sorrow and yet place their hands in His. This God is the One who leans down and kisses away the tears, who bandages up our emotional wounds, tying together the parts within us that are broken in order to make us whole again. He is the God of bleeding hands and feet who knows our sorrow better than anyone else ever could.

Healing Lord, bring me the medicine of Your love. Bind up what is broken within me. I want to be whole in You. Amen.

Hungry

*"If you spend yourselves in behalf of the hungry and
satisfy the needs of the oppressed, then your light will rise
in the darkness, and your night will become like the noonday."*
ISAIAH 58:10

Is there any crime, any sin, any heartache in the world that is not somehow linked to hunger? When people are hungry for food, they sometimes get so desperate that they will do anything for a shred of satisfaction. They will even steal from other hungry people. When people are feeding an addiction, they have a gnawing hole in their bodies and brains that cries out for more every day. When people are hungry for love, they sometimes look past all boundaries in order to take hold of anything that resembles affection. And when people are hungry for power, they greedily consume anyone in their path to get more of it.

In the book of Isaiah, the Lord speaks through His prophet to His people. In chapter 58, God rebukes the people for their inconsistencies. He says people come to Him, claiming their devotion, seeming as if they want to follow Him—they even fast, making themselves hungry on purpose in order to show their dedication. But God points out that the fasting they do is only that—a show. They are not really sacrificing anything. They are not giving up control and submitting themselves to God's will. Instead, they are still holding on tight to their power, exploiting their workers and quarreling with one another over their supposed rights.

The kind of fasting God wants is the kind that leads to change. It's the kind of hunger for Him that results in chains of injustice being broken to set people free. It's the kind of hunger that gives up meals not to feed one's self-image but to feed every last person made in the image of God. It's the kind of hunger that isn't satisfied until every person has shelter, until everyone has a place to call home (see verses 6–7).

Hunger can lead to crime and sin and heartache. But hunger for God can lead to honor and generosity and love. Hunger for God helps us stand out in a world of people clamoring for a spotlight and makes us shine, reflecting the Light that came down and dwelt in our darkness. Hunger for God can bring about a satisfaction that is deeper and fuller than any meal could ever produce.

*Lord, make me hungry for You and for Your Word.
I want to feast on Your wisdom and love. Amen.*

Bought at a Price

You are not your own; you were bought at a price.
Therefore honor God with your bodies.
1 Corinthians 6:19–20

. . . .

Many of us these days resist the idea of being bought. There are all kinds of connotations of that phrase, "bought at a price," that make us feel uncomfortable. We might think of slaves standing on an auction block. Or we might think of prostitutes standing on a street corner. It's funny how we will pay for objects and then consider them valuable, but when we pay for people we consider them worth less than others. Or perhaps the value is assigned based on what a person is being paid to do. When we pay for people to do manual labor—to offer their bodies to do the work of some of the dirtiest jobs we know of—we consider the people equal to the value of the dirt.

But when Jesus paid for us, He was not setting the price based on what we could or could not do for Him. He valued us because of who we are. And who are we?

We are His brothers and sisters. We are children of God. We are members of a royal priesthood. We are cherished citizens in the kingdom of the King above all kings. We are bearers of His image and His light. We are the vessels of His Spirit.

We are temples. We are places where God comes to meet His people and speak to them. We are homes for Him to dwell in. We are the centers from which worship flows back to Him. We are His creation, His precious possessions, His loved ones. We are priceless to Him. And because of that, He paid everything to have us.

And because of all of that, we must be careful about what and whom we unite ourselves with. Paul writes to the Corinthians about their sexual practices not because there is anything wrong with sex. On the contrary, God designed sex to be one of those things that we can consider beneficial. Sex within the design of God is a gift, resulting in holy unions and producing blessings, sometimes precious little blessings wrapped in joy. But sex outside of His plan—sex for the sake of sex, sex practiced as part of idolatry, or as a way of oppression, or as a form of abuse, or as a replacement for the love of Christ, or as a meaningless act—does not bring blessing. Instead, it separates us from Him.

We were bought at a price—we are worth something to God. And we should act like it.

Lord, help me to know I am valuable. Amen.

Knowledge

Knowing isn't everything.
1 CORINTHIANS 8:7 MSG

. . . .

Remember that time when you were young and knew it all? Remember when you thought your parents didn't understand anything about the world and you couldn't possibly explain it to them? Remember when you were an expert on life? Remember when you couldn't be bothered to take anyone's advice unless it agreed with your own opinions? Remember when you thought you had it all figured out?

Maybe you were five. Maybe you were fifteen. Maybe you were fifty-five. Maybe this was never you. Or maybe this describes you right now.

Most of us go through some period of our lives when we think we've cornered the market on some type of knowledge. And because we think we know something, we then become judges of those who do not—and we generally decide that almost everyone else knows nothing. That's when the trouble begins. Because if you get stuck in this kind of thinking, you also get in the habit of not listening to others. Eventually you just don't think about others at all, because you are too busy consulting yourself.

In this first letter to the Corinthians, Paul keeps having to remind these believers about who they are and why that matters. As human beings often do, these people of Corinth kept getting distracted with trivial matters, and then they let those distractions create divisions. They forgot what they were supposed to know was true.

Here Paul calls them back to truth again. He says, "We never really know enough until we recognize that God alone knows it all" (verse 3 MSG). He tells them not to be so concerned with what they are eating, or indeed, with anything they are doing, that they forget the kind of people they are supposed to be. Not "know-it-alls who treat others as know-nothings," but people who are "sensitive to the fact that we're not all at the same level of understanding" (verse 7 MSG).

Knowing things is good. Knowing how to follow God is great. But knowing isn't everything. We have to remember to love too. We have to remember to listen. We have to remember to be humble. And we have to remember the One who is the source of all useful knowledge we could ever hope to have.

♥　·　♥　·　♥　·　♥

God, help me not to be so full of knowledge that I forget to listen and love.
I want to listen to what You have to tell me and love others as You would
love them. Help me, please. Keep me humble. Amen.

The Trouble with Lukewarm

"I know your works, that you are neither cold nor hot."
REVELATION 3:15 NKJV

. . . .

It's the kind of water you put a baby in—gentle, relaxing, even soothing. Not too hot, not too cold. Just right in the middle. Not a shock to the system and not painful. Nothing extreme or radical. Nothing unsettling.

It's just the right kind of atmosphere for a baby. But we are not babies. We are meant to be grown. And growing.

In John's vision that he details in the book of Revelation, he hears Jesus giving messages to a list of various churches. These are groups of believers—people who are supposed to be walking in the steps of Christ. But several of these churches had some serious problems, not unlike many of our churches today.

The church of the Laodiceans is often referred to as the "lukewarm church." And just in case you were wondering, that isn't a compliment. They were not being praised by Christ for their ability to stay neutral or for their diplomatic prowess. They were not being complimented on the calm, steady nature of their faith. No, instead Jesus said, "I will vomit you out of My mouth" (verse 16 NKJV). Like soup that has cooled down after sitting too long on the table, the people of Laodicea had left a bad taste in the mouth of God.

Why had they become this way? Jesus gives us the clue. "Because you say, 'I am rich, have become wealthy, and have need of nothing'—and do not know that you are wretched, miserable, poor, blind, and naked" (verse 17 NKJV). Be careful here to note that it was not the fact that the Laodiceans were wealthy that was the problem. The problem was that they had become too proud to see what they lacked. And in their pride, they had become complacent.

The trouble with lukewarm is that the only natural way to go from there is colder. Lukewarm water doesn't get hot on its own. It just continues to cool down. The Laodiceans, in their blindness, had lost their passion for God. But all was not lost. Jesus rebuked them, but it was a merciful rebuke—advising them to set the bar higher, to become refined, to test themselves with courage and purity, and to open their eyes to all they yet could be in Christ.

Jesus stands at the door and knocks for us too. Will you open the door to Him and listen to what He has to say? Go ahead. Do it. Dine with the Savior. Just don't serve Him cold soup.

Lord, I want to live my life on fire for You. Amen.

How Much More

How much more, then, will the blood of Christ, who through the eternal Spirit offered himself unblemished to God, cleanse our consciences from acts that lead to death, so that we may serve the living God!
HEBREWS 9:14

The dog hides in the corner, head down, tail nervously wagging. In the kitchen, the remains of last night's dinner, pulled out of the trash and strewn about the newly mopped floor, wait to welcome the dog's master home.

"Bad dog. What did you do?"

The big pup pushes into the corner a little more tightly, acting for all the world as if he knows he is guilty. And perhaps he does. We cannot really know what goes on in the minds of animals. We cannot read their thoughts. Some pets seem to understand the connection, at least in the short term, of their actions with habitual consequences. That is, good behavior gets rewarded with treats; bad behavior gets punished by time out in the corner or by a verbal reprimand. But even the smartest dogs do not seem to carry around with them the weight of years of mistakes and sins—doggy guilt.

But we do. Many of us find that one of the hardest tasks as Christians is to truly believe that we are forgiven—that our records can be wiped clean. Instead, we make daily sacrifices, supposed deals with our Lord and Savior that are more like New Year's resolutions (with just about as much follow-through success): "If I pray every day, God will forgive me for being a rebellious child." Or "I will read my Bible and volunteer at church; then God will overlook all my little white lies."

Some of us just go ahead and put ourselves in the corner. We dole out our punishments—taking ourselves out of certain opportunities or holding back from being fully alive in Christ. We tuck our tails and hide, fearful of our Master's voice.

But nothing we do can cleanse our hearts. It's worth saying that again: *Nothing we do can cleanse our hearts.* Only Jesus can do that. Only His sacrifice can atone for us. But what a sacrifice! And what a Savior! He can do so much more for us than just relieve us from guilt. He can do so much more than we could ever hope to achieve through our self-rebuke. He can equip us and empower us to serve the living God!

Lord Jesus, help me to believe in You more and more.
Help me to trust that Your blood was enough for me. Amen.

Working It Out

The LORD God took the man and put him in the
Garden of Eden to work it and take care of it.
GENESIS 2:15

. . . .

Thomas Edison, the famous Midwestern inventor of the electric lightbulb and many other creations, is quoted as saying, "Opportunity is missed by most people because it is dressed in overalls and looks like work." He was certainly not a man who shied away from work. His life story is a tale of taking advantage of every opportunity he had to experiment and try out his new ideas—even when it sometimes cost him whatever current job he was employed at. He is a great example of the spark of the Creator that is in each of us—that desire within us to make things, to care for our world, and to figure out solutions to problems.

When we are in the middle of difficult times, it is good to remember who made us, and what He made us to do. As Christians, we believe we were formed by God. God formed man from "the dust of the ground and breathed into his nostrils the breath of life, and the man became a living being" (Genesis 2:7). We are the work of God, and He created us in His image—in the image of the Master Craftsman, with skill in our hands and innovation in our hearts. It's no wonder that, especially when we are experiencing hard situations and complicated feelings, we feel better when we are doing productive work.

The first man and the first woman were no different than we are in this respect. Certainly they wouldn't have been content with just wandering about in the garden aimlessly. They must have been grateful to have been given a job to do. And what an honor! The Creator of all trusted them to take care of His creation. Not only did they enjoy the work of tending the garden, but God saw that humans would thrive in the work of tending relationships. He declared, "It is not good for the man to be alone" (verse 18). Men and women grow and flourish through relationships with one another—through the endless pursuit of understanding and learning from one another and figuring out how to live together.

But even after the Fall, when man and woman had disobeyed God, God in His mercy did not take meaningful work away from us. It's true that with the curse came pain and sorrow—work would never be easy—but God in His wisdom knew that we would find blessings even within the curse.

Lord, when I don't know what else to do,
help me to work for You. Amen.

My Rock

"The LORD is my rock, my fortress and my deliverer;
my God is my rock, in whom I take refuge."
2 SAMUEL 22:2–3

The little boy curled his fingers around the edge of what to him seemed like a small mountain. With every bit of strength he had in his chubby legs and sweaty hands, he pushed himself up on his toes and pulled his body up, up, up on top of the large, sun-warmed rock. At last. He let out a whoosh of relief and spread himself out on the massive flat face of the stone, face up, eyes closed, soaking in the golden light.

Up on the rock, he didn't worry about the neighbor's scary miniature poodle that always nipped at his heels when he ran too close to it. He didn't have to be afraid of anything. And he didn't even have to think too much about being tagged "it." No one could see him there on the rock, especially when he made himself as flat as could be. The rock was his safe place. It was where he liked to come when he thought his parents were being unfair. It was where he came when he felt sad or alone, like when his favorite goldfish died. No one would have guessed how comforting a giant rock could be, but this little boy knew.

Have you ever found comfort and rest in an unlikely place? Maybe you have a friend who's gruff and intimidating on the outside, but has a heart of gold on the inside. Maybe you have a favorite spot in your town that seems ugly to anyone else, but gives you peace. Maybe you have found quiet in the middle of chaos or found refreshment in a desert landscape. Maybe you find soothing in a storm.

David had known a lot of storms. He described the "waves of death" circling him and the "torrents of destruction" overwhelming him (2 Samuel 22:5). But then he called out to God, and what was God's response? "The earth trembled and quaked, the foundations of the heavens shook; they trembled because he was angry" (verse 8). But God was not angry with David—no, God rebuked David's enemies, using all the imposing gloom of thunder and the echoes of His might. Because David was faithful, God showed faithfulness to him. And because God is the almighty, all-powerful rock of a God that He is, His faithfulness is strong and loud and formidable. And in that, we can find comfort.

Lord, when I am shaken, help me
hold tight to the solid reality of You. Amen.

Mightier than the Sea

Mightier than the thunder of the great waters, mightier
than the breakers of the sea—the LORD on high is mighty.
PSALM 93:4

. . . .

"The seas have lifted up, LORD" (verse 3). . .

It's one of those days. You know the kind. The schedules are conflicting. The family members are quarreling. The colleagues are circling. The deadlines are overwhelming. And you are barely swimming. Or are you almost drowning?

"The seas have lifted up their voice" (verse 3).

What is it that comes to your mind? Echoes of defeatist thinking? Guilt-ridden nightmares of despair? Accusations of unmet expectations? Predictions of failure? Or can you hear words of encouragement yet floating high on the crashing waves? Can you hear truth that comes from the source of all truth? Can you hear that you are loved? That no matter what mess you are swirling in right now, the One who made you has you in His hands?

"The seas have lifted up their pounding waves" (verse 3).

Truth is heavy. Praise is weighty. Sometimes accepting the vision God has for you, for your life, is hard to do. It's hard to grasp the idea that someone so big, so important, so amazing, cares so much about what happens to you—on this day, in this town, at this moment, right now. His words come pounding down on us—but we are not left beaten. When ocean waves crash into us, they may well leave us breathless—but not lifeless. On the contrary, when that saltwater comes for us, we feel more alive, not less. We want to get up and chase the waves away, far away, to lands unknown beyond the horizon. We want to swim with schools of fish and become friends with dolphins. We want to breathe deeply, know deeply, love deeply.

"Mightier than the thunder of the great waters, mightier than the breakers of the sea—the LORD on high is mighty" (verse 4).

Our God is mighty—deep and wide like the ocean. Unpredictable and beyond our control. We cannot fathom Him. We cannot contain Him. We can only begin to grasp the words to describe Him. He reaches into our lives like the tides—sometimes arriving quickly and full-on, with beautiful, high, rushing waves of light. Sometimes He stretches out into our days—steady and strong and serene, teaching us peace and patience and calm.

The seas have lifted up their voice and we have heard it. And now we can join them in their song: "The Lord, our Lord—our Lord on high is mighty."

Sometimes, Lord, just knowing You are here, as surely as I know
the seas will come to shore, is enough to bring me peace. Amen.

No Condemnation

There is therefore now no condemnation to those who are in Christ Jesus,
who do not walk according to the flesh, but according to the Spirit.
ROMANS 8:1 NKJV

Remember that first time you were caught red-handed—maybe with your hand actually stuck right down in that cookie jar? Maybe you were teasing the cat, and that last pull to the tail led to you being marked with a claw-written signature you wouldn't soon forget. Maybe you were caught in a lie, wound up in the sticky mess of your own deceit. Or maybe you were caught hurting someone else, and the pain on their face told the whole story before you could even get out a "But. . ."

No condemnation? Not likely, right? Not in your corner of the world. When you got caught, you received a quick judgment and sentence, complete with disapproving stare from your mom or dad, or that mean old babysitter.

We're used to being judged. Maybe that's why we so easily fall into judging others. But we are not, in general, well suited to that job. We bring with us too many prejudices, too many experiences that color our conclusions. Too many times we judge in ignorance, without getting the full picture. And what's even worse, we judge without mercy.

The only One who is perfectly qualified to be our judge is Jesus. And yet He is the One who spares us the punishment we actually deserve. Instead of finding us guilty, as He rightfully could do, He takes on our guilt. Instead of pointing out our faults, He takes on our wounds. Instead of showering us with a barrage of rebuke and condemnation, He rains down blessing through the Spirit.

Jesus Christ, who has no earthly reason to show us mercy, demonstrates for us the perfect power of heavenly thinking. He loves without condition. He gives without getting. He offers without being asked. He pardons without punishing.

No condemnation. Consider those words to be your life slogan. How is your life different, or how should it be different, with the knowledge that you are free from condemnation? You never have to face hell, because Jesus faced it for you. You can know without a doubt that your life here on earth is just a dot on an eternal line, and you get to live out the rest of that line in the freedom and glory of heaven.

No condemnation. How does that knowledge shape the way you look at others? How can you extend the mercy Jesus has shown you and share the freedom of those two words with someone else today?

Lord, I know I may get in all kinds of trouble,
but praise God that You offer me no condemnation. Amen.

Bottom

"We shall see what will become of his dreams!"
GENESIS 37:20 NKJV

- -

How in the world did I get here?

Joseph must have been bewildered. At the beginning of this chapter of his life, he is on top of the world, a favorite of his father, respected, and seemingly favored by God. He'd had dreams indicating that even his older brothers and father, members of the family of the great patriarch Abraham, would bow down to him—young Joseph.

And now he was stuck at the bottom of a pit, sitting in the dirt, with literally nowhere to go.

Nowhere to go, that is, but up.

Sometimes we just don't see how God is with us until we've hit bottom. Now, this doesn't mean we should aim for bottom, just so we can experience Immanuel ("God with us") even more. As Paul said, "What shall we say then? Shall we continue in sin that grace may abound? Certainly not!" (Romans 6:1–2 NKJV). After all, Joseph never intended to end up in that dry well. He didn't throw himself in there.

But one wonders, as he was down there in the dark, disrobed, listening to the harsh voices of his brothers somewhere overhead, did Joseph wake up to the reality that perhaps he had allowed his own pride to blur his vision? Had he become so content in his position of favor that he hadn't seen the growing divide between him and his brothers? How had he missed all the signs of their anger?

It's all too easy when things are going well—when we feel as though we are sitting on top of the world—to forget to be sensitive to the perspectives of others. We can't control how people feel about us, but we can try to be better listeners. We don't have to hide when good things happen to us, but we can be sensitive and respectful in the way we share our news, and we can give the glory and our thanks to God.

The grown man we know as Joseph is someone we all look to as an example of great faith, perseverance, and forgiveness. But young Joseph is the picture of a self-absorbed teenager—annoying his family with his ignorance and arrogance.

As Joseph sat there, stripped and bruised, he had limited options. But one thing he could do was pray. He could look up to the light and ask God to be with him in the darkness. And God certainly was there with Joseph. God stayed with Joseph all his life.

And God is with you too—whether you are basking in the light or hunkering in the dark.

*Lord, help me to see You with me all the time—
even when it looks like I have nowhere to go. Amen.*

Unloved, Beloved

I will call Not My People, My People,
and she who is Unloved, Beloved.
ROMANS 9:25 CSB

. . . .

The mutt sat shivering in the corner, on the edge of a puddle of his own making. From his looks, he seemed to be one weird mixture—part Chihuahua, part pug, part Lab, and part some kind of terrier, perhaps? It was anyone's guess. One snaggletooth protruded up over his top lip, where a wiry set of whiskers gave him the quirky impression of having a mustache. His eyes bulged out from his tiny head. He snuffled and sputtered as he breathed. One leg stuck straight out from underneath his belly, as if even his own limbs were trying to escape this creature.

His coloring was mottled—some combination of black, gray, and brown that made him look as though he had just bathed in a mud puddle. But he hadn't bathed at all—maybe ever. The stench of wet dog rose up from him like the mushroom cloud of an odor bomb.

And all around him bounded a family of happy, fluffy, handsome golden retriever pups.

He was definitely not the pick of the litter.

He wasn't even from this litter.

But the little girl who walked into the shelter that day saw him all alone in the corner and walked right over to him, not paying attention to the bouncy balls of golden fur running all about. She held out her hand, and the unlovely creature snuffled, stuck out his tongue, and licked her fingers, then looked up at her with his big eyes and wagged his tail.

"This one, Mommy!"

Maybe you feel like you aren't exactly the pick of the litter. Maybe you feel left out and unloved. Maybe you feel that way because that has been part of your experience.

But our God delights in the lesser things of this world. He takes pleasure in exalting the humbled. He enjoys shining a spotlight on what has previously been hidden in the shadows. He makes "known the riches of his glory on objects of mercy" (Romans 9:23 CSB). God takes the forgotten ones of the world—the broken, the unholy, the used up, the horrid, the ugly—and He remembers them, heals them, sanctifies them, restores them, and transforms them. He uses unexpected people to bring to fruition the fruits of His glory.

God can and will use you—no matter what you look like or feel like, or what your life has been like to this point. And not only will He use you to do great things in His kingdom; He will love you.

♥ • ♥ • ♥ •

Beloved God, thank You for loving me,
even when I feel unlovable. Amen.

Mind Your Own Business

*Make it your goal to live a quiet life, minding your own business
and working with your hands, just as we instructed you before.*
1 Thessalonians 4:11 nlt

We might call it caring for our neighbors. We might call it being friendly. We might call it our civic duty.

But let's face it—sometimes we are just using those terms as a cover-up for something less. . .loving. Sometimes we are just being nosy. Sometimes we are just inserting ourselves where we don't belong.

And sometimes we are doing all of that, then judging others on top of it.

But what we don't realize at the time is that we also are being judged. We who are believers are being watched by the world. People have heard us claim to believe in a God of mercy and peace and love. They've heard us invite them to church—"Come as you are! We accept everyone! Jesus loves everyone!" And yet they know we've never invited them to dinner.

They hear us claim to pray for others and to care about others, but they don't see us out in the trenches, rolling up our sleeves and helping people. They hear us say that everyone is equally important in the eyes of God. But they see us posting messages on our social media pages that clearly indicate that some of us are better than others—some of us know the truth, and everyone else is stupid.

How often do we stop and think about what our actions look like to those who do not know God? Consider for a moment everything you've done today. Where in your day could someone look and find God? Where could they find you giving glory to Him? Take a look at the things you've said out loud or online. Which words represent the Gospel of Jesus well? Which ones don't? Which ones offer a confusing view of Christianity to those who are outside of it?

No one says we have to live perfect lives. But the goal is to live quietly. Yes, we can have personality and speak out at appropriate times, but we are meant to live in such a way that our voices do not drown out the voices of others. We are meant to work hard and pay attention to the jobs we have to do. If we are good stewards of what God has given us to do, people will see that we are reliable and trustworthy. And being trustworthy in our own lives will make them more likely to trust what we have to say to them about life in Christ.

Lord, help my life to be a good example of Your love. Amen.

Exercise of Hope

*For physical training is of some value, but godliness has value for all things,
holding promise for both the present life and the life to come.*
1 Timothy 4:8

Up, down. Up, down. Fifty squats—done. Up, down. Up, down. Ten pull-ups—done. Run, jump, jog, walk. Sweat. Breathe. Breathe some more. Drink water. Cool down. Lie down. Rest. Repeat.

Following a physical regimen creates a pattern in your life—a settled expectation of what is to come. This pattern makes it easier to keep going. When distractions arise, you have a commitment already established. If you miss a day, you really do miss it. Your body misses it.

Physical training is good not only for the body but for the mind. Study after study shows that physical exercise is an effective part of treating mental health issues. Exercise can lift someone out of depression and stabilize moods. People with ongoing medical conditions have been able to reduce or even get rid of medications simply by increasing the number of minutes they spend each week moving their bodies around.

And while physical training certainly does have all these benefits, the practice of godliness is even more rewarding. Godliness is an exercise of hope. It's a way of training our hearts and minds to be focused on the life to come—our life with God in the eternal home He is preparing for us. As we focus on that heavenly kingdom, we begin to want more and more to live in a way that pleases our heavenly King.

But how do we practice godliness? What are the exercises of the soul? Paul gives us some ideas. "Devote yourself to the public reading of Scripture, to preaching and to teaching" (1 Timothy 4:13). You don't have to be a preacher or Sunday school teacher to do this—you can get together with your family or friends to read and discuss the Bible together. Talking about God's Word together makes it come alive and helps you gain new perspectives you might not see on your own. Paul also advises Timothy to "set an example for the believers in speech, in conduct, in love, in faith and in purity" (verse 12). If you want to get better at anything, just consider who might be watching you and how you want to impact them. The challenge of setting an example in godliness will cause you to want to be a better imitator of Christ.

Paul also challenges Timothy to persevere in these exercises, "because if you do, you will save both yourself and your hearers" (verse 16). Physical training might improve your health, but training in godliness can save your soul through Christ.

Jesus, be my godliness Trainer. Amen.

Come to Me

"Come to Me, all you who labor and are
heavy laden, and I will give you rest."
MATTHEW 11:28 NKJV

. . . .

On good days, Sam comes home from work in the evening and greets his wife and children. He solicitously asks about each of their days, catching up on all the activities and news reports. But lately, there aren't too many of these good days.

Work at the plant has been dropping for months, and there are steady rumors about layoffs. Although Sam has been at the company for more years than many others, he hasn't been there long enough to withstand the absence of work. Sam worries. He comes home, and he has a glass of wine to relax. Every once in a blue moon it occurs to him to put himself in God's hands. He prays, but only rarely. More often, he wonders what will happen to him and his charges; he sleeps fretfully.

Bill works for the same company, and he too is plagued by worries and doubts, which he shares with his wife. But Bill has another help: he comes home each evening, and after his greetings, he takes time by himself to reflect on his day.

On one such evening, he recalls a recent Sunday service at which he heard the pastor read: "Come to Me, all you who labor and are heavy laden, and I will give you rest." He remembers and smiles to himself. *I certainly labor and am heavy laden*, he muses. *So it sounds like Jesus is sending an invitation to me.* He closes his eyes and asks Jesus to help him with his fears about work, about bills, and about all the craziness in the world. He asks Jesus to help him find a way forward that will be helpful and assuring to his family.

After a while, he feels a nudge, and he opens his eyes to find his wife standing there looking at him with a smile playing on her lips. "Why are you smiling at me?" he asks.

"I was just about to ask you about that smile on your face," she says in response. "I've been standing here for about a minute, watching you sitting there like the cat that ate the canary, as if you don't have a care in the world."

"Oh, I have cares, all right," he replies, standing up. "I have cares, good cares, like you and the kids." And holding her close, he rocks her slightly in an embrace and gives thanks to Jesus for a few moments of peace and rest and a lightening of his burden.

"For my yoke is easy to bear, and the burden I give you is light" (verse 30 NLT).

♥ · · ♥ · · . ♥ · ·

Lord, thank You for the invitation. I will come. Amen.

Refuge of Destruction

Come, see the glorious works of the LORD:
See how he brings destruction upon the world.
PSALM 46:8 NLT

There's a scene in the film *Superman* (1978) in which the hero throws a green crystal, and out of an Arctic landscape, through crackling glacial slabs, shards of ice burst forth, exploding into a frozen sky. The Fortress of Solitude, the superhero's elaborate (and chilly) man cave, rises up like some kind of fantastic Nordic crown for a giant ice princess.

The fortress is Superman's home base—his palace of refuge. It's a place where he can go to find safety and seclusion. It's a place where he can be reconnected to his source. But this quiet, hidden sanctuary is born out of crashing destruction.

Sometimes when the certainty of our life circumstances is collapsing around us, and the solid ground we thought we were standing on seems as shifting and unsteady as the sandy shore under the ocean waves, that is when we find our real source of strength. We cannot hold too tightly to the things of this earth—the things that perish and fade away. But we can hold on forever to God, and know He will hold on forever to us.

Nations have been in chaos before. Long ago, kingdoms fought one another and castles crumbled to the ground. Governments have fallen apart. But where God dwells, we can take refuge. And the Lord of Heaven's Armies is right here—here among us.

But this is not a refuge of quiet and calm. This is the place where God brings destruction. "He causes wars to end throughout the earth. He breaks the bow and snaps the spear; he burns the shields with fire" (Psalm 46:9 NLT). The God of peace, who destroys the weapons of violence and rules over nations, calls out to us, "Be still" (verse 10). He tells us to be silent in our actions and our speech—but not so we will do nothing at all. Not so we can just be spectators of His might. "Be still, and know that I am God! I will be honored by every nation. I will be honored throughout the world" (verse 10 NKJV).

How can we know that He is God? We have to ask. We have to do research. We have to search the scriptures and see who God claims to be, what He is like, what He does, and whom He does it to. We have to keep searching and talking about Him in every corner of the world. We can meet others and tell them about Him. And then we can be still—still in the satisfaction of knowing who He is and what He wants from us.

God, please bring peace out of the destruction in our lives. Amen.

New Life

For you have been born again, but not to a life that will quickly end. Your new life will last forever because it comes from the eternal, living word of God.
1 PETER 1:23 NLT

. . . .

She sighed deeply as she sank down into her armchair, kicked off her shoes, and put her feet up on the ottoman. *What a day.* She rubbed her forehead and closed her eyes. The headaches never seemed to go away long enough for her to think straight. They certainly made it hard for her to concentrate—especially in a classroom full of twenty-eight talkative first graders.

She thought about what the doctor had told her a week ago. It all seemed like a bad dream. She couldn't fathom the idea that she might have only a short time left to live on this earth. She knew there had to be more tests and exams and second opinions, but no matter what came of it all, her perspective had shifted for good.

Life was short. She needed to really live it. *Every day.*

She reached for the Bible on the table next to her and turned to the spot where she had left off reading that morning. "People are like grass; their beauty is like a flower in the field. The grass withers and the flower fades. But the word of the Lord remains forever" (1 Peter 1:24–25 NLT).

She remembered how she had been struck by those words: *Withers. . .fades. I don't want to wither and fade*, she had thought.

"I won't." The sound of her own voice startled her. Her eyes ran back up through the verses until she found what she was looking for.

"Now we live with great expectation, and we have a priceless inheritance. . .beyond the reach of change and decay. . . . So be truly glad. There is wonderful joy ahead, even though you must endure many trials for a little while. . . . Rejoice with a glorious, inexpressible joy. The reward for trusting him will be the salvation of your souls" (verses 3–4, 6, 8–9 NLT).

That was how she wanted to live—like her salvation depended on it. She wanted to be glad and rejoice. She wanted to remember that God's Word has promised us a priceless inheritance, and His Word never fails. It goes on and on—forever. Just like she would go on and on with Him—forever. Her old life might be marked by disease and death—but she was living in the new life now. And there was wonderful joy ahead.

Lord God, Giver of life, help me trust Your promises for my new life, even when I walk through some of life's hardest trials. Amen.

Go in Peace

Jesus said to the woman,
"Your faith has saved you; go in peace."
Luke 7:50

Ellie had been in bad situations before. In fact, she had made bad decisions repeatedly, but nothing that had happened to her fazed her very much. She had gone through innumerable punitive cycles of withheld allowances, confiscated cell phones, lost privileges, restrictions on where she could go and who she could hang out with, and so forth. In the course of time, she had seen it all. Or so she thought.

Now she was sitting in the principal's outer office, waiting for her parents to arrive. Ellie and two other students had been caught in possession of drugs, and she had been told that she was going to be expelled from school. *Expelled.*

It didn't matter that her parents would be angry; no, they would be devastated. Although she didn't mind giving them a hard time, she didn't want to hurt them—especially her mother. Ellie thought hard about what she would say. *It wasn't that big a deal, just some weed. Everybody does it on occasion.* No one in the principal's office would even look at her. She was lost, not worth a glance. Suddenly, for the first time in her life, Ellie felt ashamed. Surprising even herself, she started to cry. And at the same time that she started to cry, she felt suddenly afraid. What was going to happen to her?

And in that moment of feeling lost and alone and afraid, she blurted out, "Jesus, oh God, help me. I don't want to be thrown out. Please, help me." As she was weeping to herself, the door to the office opened and her parents walked in. Reflexively, she ran to embrace her mother, saying over and over again how sorry she was. "They're going to throw me out," she kept repeating. Try as she might, Ellie could not stop crying.

Her father reached for her. He turned her face up to him and looked in her eyes. She was shaking with sobs. She thought he was probably completely fed up with her. What would be her punishment this time? But as she clutched on to him, her father's arms wrapped around her, and he pressed her head against his chest and said, "Hush up, Ellie. Whatever you did, it's not the end of the world. It may be the end of this school. . .but not the end of the world. Stop crying." As her sobs began to subside, he asked her, "Are you really sorry now, Ellie? Are you going to stop?"

She nodded against him, mumbling, "Yes."

"Well then, God will forgive you. And I forgive you. Let's be at peace together."

Lord, help me to remember the extent of Your forgiveness. Amen.

Lost and Found

"And when she finds it, she calls her friends and neighbors together and says, 'Rejoice with me; I have found my lost coin.' "
Luke 15:9

Keys. Socks. Homework. Bills. Ten dollars. Grocery list. Your marbles.

Undoubtedly, this could be a list of lost things in many people's households. Why do we lose things so easily? We're headed out the door in the morning, bag on shoulder, coffee in hand, to-do list in mind, and then suddenly we stop. *Keys. Where are the keys?* They were in our hands just a minute ago. We can see them in our mind's eye, but our real eyes can't seem to find them. The frantic search of the whole house begins. Couch cushions turned over. Papers lifted up. Purses and pockets turned inside out. Cupboards checked—just for good measure. And then, where do we find them? Right on the key hook, where they always are.

Perhaps this scene is familiar to you. Or maybe it reminds you of something else you misplace often. Or maybe it reminds you of someone else in your household.

Are you the loser or the finder of things? When something is lost in your house, does everyone come to you, expecting you to find it—whatever it is? Or when something is lost, do fingers point at you—blaming you for hiding some object that you never even knew existed before this moment?

That experience of sudden realization of the absence of some necessary (or at least significant) item is pretty common to the human experience. Surely each one of us has lost things. Maybe we've even lost something very important to us—either a thing that has sentimental value or a thing that is needed as a practical matter. We all know that frustration, that sense of momentary helplessness, that irritation with ourselves because we can't just make things appear at will. Moreover, we probably all know the annoyance or even grief at having lost something important that we just cannot recover.

In those moments, when we've searched absolutely everywhere we can think of and still come up empty, we can feel a little empty ourselves. We can feel a little like we are the lost things. And we want to be found. We want to be restored to a place where we know who we are, and we know what we've done, and we know where we are going next.

Thanks to God, we can never be lost in His kingdom. Even when we try to hide, He comes to us. He restores us. He reminds us exactly how important we are to Him. And He leads us back to where we need to be going.

Lord of the lost, keep finding me. Amen.

A Burden Too Heavy

My guilt has overwhelmed me
like a burden too heavy to bear.
PSALM 38:4

David was no perfect saint. Although he is called "a man after [God's] own heart" (Acts 13:22), the shepherd boy who became king of Israel committed many sins as he traveled on the path to following God's will. When we consider the weight of his guilt burden, we think about things like lust, greed, deceit, adultery, and murder.

His was a heavy load to bear.

Perhaps we are comparing our own load to David's and thinking, *Well, at least I'm not as bad as all that.* But sin is sin. And whether we have committed one seemingly small act of darkness or many such acts—that darkness still casts a shadow on our hearts.

We are changed when we sin. And the more we get caught up in sin, the harder it is for us to keep walking under that burden of guilt and shame and darkness.

David speaks of sin like an illness: "Because of your wrath there is no health in my body; there is no soundness in my bones because of my sin" (Psalm 38:3). "My back is filled with searing pain," he says; "I am feeble and utterly crushed; I groan in anguish of heart" (verses 7–8).

He also talks about the consequences of this sin spreading out to the people around him. "Neighbors stay far away," perhaps keeping their distance to avoid being tainted themselves by David's reputation (verse 11). Even friends and companions avoid him—they don't know what to do with the king who seems to be stuck in his own dungeon. And as David's friends move away, his enemies close in—sensing his weakness and plotting his demise.

David confesses that he even feels like his own testimony has been stripped from him. He can't speak—he can't defend himself, because he realizes he has no defense. No excuse. No reply. No reason that could justify his actions. The only thing he can do is confess to God. "I am troubled by my sin" (verse 18). Amen, David. Who among us cannot agree with his statement? We are troubled—we are changed and darkened and hurt and confined and suffocated by our sin.

But thankfully, we are still loved. Though everyone else may keep their distance, God is near. What Psalm 38 shows us most of all is that, though David was wounded and weighed down by sin, he was still seeking God—asking God to stay close. And that is why he was called a man after God's heart.

Do not be far from me, my God,
especially when I am troubled by my sin. Amen.

How Small

If you falter in a time of trouble,
how small is your strength!
PROVERBS 24:10

Picture in your mind for just a moment the strongest person you've ever seen or heard of—the person who you think has the most physical strength. Perhaps you are thinking of a bodybuilder, or a guy in the circus who can hold up ten other guys, or some amazing duodecahexathlete (yes, that might not be a real word).

How did that person get to be so strong? Surely no one comes out of the womb lifting cars or running twenty-five miles or sporting muscles that bulge out of their diapers. Strong men and women have to work up to that level. They start with small challenges and gradually work up to bigger ones, until those bigger ones seem small to them. Along the way they have setbacks. And along the way they have to stay disciplined and keep eating good food and resting and working their bodies.

In order to be strong and stay strong, they have to keep practicing being strong. They have to keep envisioning what it looks like to be even stronger. And when sickness or injuries come, they have to allow time to heal, and then they have to get right back at the work of growing stronger.

The writer of this proverb presents a scenario: we see some type of injustice, and instead of doing anything about it, we pretend not to see it (Proverbs 24:11–12). We falter. We feel afraid to speak up, so we just shrink back from the opportunity.

There may be all kinds of good reasons to be afraid. It may be that speaking up will cost us—maybe even put our own lives at risk. It may be that we don't think we can actually help. But being *afraid* to do what is right is not the problem here. Being afraid is normal. Being afraid can even be good. Being *led* by fear away from the truth is when trouble really hits us.

This is the faltering that is happening in the scenario presented by the writer of this proverb. It's not about being afraid. It's about being dishonest. It's about forgetting who we are and turning away from what is good. It's about deceiving ourselves.

To be strong, even in times of trouble, we have to practice being strong. We have to discipline ourselves to seek truth every day. We have to envision what it looks like to be a person following God's truth. At first our strength—and our faith—may be small, but with practice and discipline, it can grow into something that can stand up under enormous amounts of pressure.

Lord, challenge my strength
so I can be strong like You. Amen.

Belonging

*"I will grant peace in the land, and you will lie
down and no one will make you afraid."*
LEVITICUS 26:6

. . . .

Do you remember what it was like to walk into a new classroom for the first time? Butterflies bounced around in your belly and crawled up your windpipe, threatening to steal your breath away. Somehow excitement and anxiety and surprise and fear and confusion and wonder all whirled into a tornado inside of you that seemed as if it might burst out at any minute, knocking all those colorful educational posters right off the cement block wall.

And all you wanted to see was someone who knew you. Someone who could see you and recognize you. Someone whose eyes would light up when they saw you and who would call out your name. You wanted to belong. You wanted someone to be your partner.

In Leviticus, God gives His people, the Israelites, many commands to follow—commands to worship Him as their God and serve Him only, commands to remind them who they are and to whom they belong. And if they don't follow those commands and forget who they are, He gives them ways to come back to Him again.

God tells His people quite simply that if they follow His commands, all will be well. They will receive what they need. They will have all the food they want and live in safety (Leviticus 26:5). God will keep them secure physically by removing wild beasts from the land and by keeping war from breaking out in their country. He will give them power over their enemies, and the numbers of the Israelites will grow and grow (verses 6–9).

But more than that, God makes them promises that set their hearts at rest. He says He will keep His covenant with them. He says He will dwell among them and walk among them and be their God. "And you will be my people" (verse 12). He reminds them that He knows them—He was the One who brought them out of Egypt. He has not forgotten them.

Whenever we walk into an uncomfortable or foreign situation, we can be assured of one thing. No matter how anxious or confused or scared we might feel, we can know for certain that when we look around the room, God is there. He is there with us. He is there for us. And He is lighting up, delighted to see us and ready to call out our name.

*Lord, I'm nervous about entering a new situation.
Help me to remember that You are looking out for me. Amen.*

Making Our Own Trouble

*"I will not rule over you, nor will my son rule
over you. The LORD will rule over you."*
JUDGES 8:23

. . . .

"Make Gideon do it—you know he's not doing anything important." "Gideon! You messed up again. All you do is make mistakes!" "Gideon, you'll never amount to anything."

One wonders what Gideon's childhood must have been like. Somewhere along the way, he got sold on the idea that he was not so special. Perhaps it was just a known status among the tribes of his people. Perhaps his family had done something that made them the butt of Israel's jokes. Or perhaps Gideon had an inferiority complex of his own creation. But when an angel came to speak to Gideon, Gideon's first reaction was not fear or even great wonder at the angel's appearance. No, Gideon's first thought was to complain: "If the LORD is with us, why has all this happened to us? Where are all his wonders. . . ?" (Judges 6:13).

The Lord was persistent. He said He was sending Gideon to save Israel out of Midian's hand. But again, Gideon seemed confused and incredulous: "How can I save Israel? My clan is the weakest in Manasseh, and I am the least in my family" (Judges 6:15). Gideon proceeded to ask for several assurances from God to be certain of God's identity. And God continued to stretch and challenge Gideon's faith by giving him increasingly hard tasks to complete.

Even when God had given Midian into Gideon's hands and rescued the Israelites, Gideon still wanted some tangible symbol of God's support. The Israelites had asked him to rule over them, and Gideon had rightly acknowledged that God was their ruler. That's where he should have stopped. But Gideon took an offering of gold earrings and made the gold into an image and placed that in his town. And that one act "became a snare to Gideon and his family" (Judges 8:27). All Israel became distracted showing honor and reverence to the idol, and after Gideon's death, the people extended their idolatry to worshipping other gods. They did not remember the Lord, and they did not remember Gideon (Judges 8:33–35).

God spoke to Gideon directly. God gave Gideon several signs. God helped Gideon lead the people to victory and then enriched Gideon's life with a huge family. But still Gideon was haunted by a feeling that he wasn't good enough to be blessed and used by God. So Gideon created his own kind of trouble in an effort to ease the insecurity he felt inside.

Remind you of anyone?

♥ ♥ ♥

*Dear Lord, let me fully rest in my
certainty of You, and nothing else. Amen.*

From Storm Wind to Whisper

He quieted the wind down to a whisper,
put a muzzle on all the big waves.
PSALM 107:29 MSG

. . . .

Praise our God, the God who makes unions out of contradictions, and knits peace out of warring factions. Praise our God for finding a path through extremes that somehow manages to be more radical than any side could imagine. And praise our God for drawing to Himself all things, small and great, known and unknown.

Psalm 107 is a psalm of praise, thanking God for the myriad ways He brings His people out of trouble. It's a beautiful, rich song that reminds us again and again that no matter where we are, what we've done, or what kind of hardship we are facing, God can rescue us. He will save us. All we have to do is call out to Him.

If we've been left high and dry by desperate times and are struggling just to get by, God will resettle us in the land of plenty. He will satisfy our thirst and feed us more than we need.

If we've been walking through a dark valley for our souls, caught up in our own rebellion and fleeing the hard work of following God's commands, God will hear our cries for help. He will grant His "miracle mercy" (verse 15 MSG) and save us from the prisons we put ourselves in.

If we've suffered physically because of bad decisions and failure to care for our bodies, God can heal us with a word—He can quiet our restlessness and give us the will to overcome our addictions.

If we've experienced a whirlwind of emotions, riding a roller coaster through personal drama, God will still our storms. He will hush the hysterical outpourings of our hearts and turn down the volume on the drama. He will quiet our wind to a whisper so we can finally hear Him speak.

This is our God—who humbles proud princes and sets them to wander without a home, while lifting up the oppressed and establishing them as overseers of flourishing estates. This is our God, who has a wisdom that confounds the scholars of this world and who has followers who seem foolish in their acts of kindness toward a world that rejects them.

"Good people see this and are glad; bad people are speechless, stopped in their tracks. If you are really wise, you'll think this over—it's time you appreciated GOD's deep love" (verses 42–43 MSG).

God, I want to swim in the depths of Your love and
experience the stillness of Your peaceful waters. Amen.

Difficult Times

Don't be naive. There are difficult times ahead.
2 TIMOTHY 3:1 MSG

With every generation, the older folks tend to look around at the younger folks and make some broad judgments: "Young people today just want to. . ." (You could fill in the blank with just about any negative behavior.) "Young people today don't value. . ." (Here, fill in the blank with any positive value the older people claim to hold dear.)

But in general, if we're all honest with ourselves, we can see that every age group has both bad characteristics and good qualities. Take a look at the list of characters Paul warns Timothy about toward the end of his second letter to his friend, and you'll probably find some familiar faces: "people are going to be self-absorbed, money-hungry, self-promoting, stuck-up, profane, contemptuous of parents, crude, coarse, dog-eat-dog, unbending, slanderers, impulsively wild, savage, cynical, treacherous, ruthless, bloated windbags, addicted to lust, and allergic to God" (2 Timothy 3:2–4 MSG).

If you look closely, you'll have to admit just about every one of us has been guilty of at least one of these negative behaviors at some point in our lives. Even if we are the best people in the world, always serving others and on fire for Jesus, who among us has not at some point been a little too fixated on what's happening in our own lives? Who hasn't lacked self-control in some area? Even when we claim to love God, who among us hasn't at some point chosen pleasure over obedience?

These things are not a young-versus-old issue. These are problems of the human heart.

Paul warns Timothy to stay away in particular from those who "make a show of religion, but behind the scenes they're animals" (verse 5 MSG). Why are these people so dangerous? Because they are the kind of people who prey on those who are weak in their faith. They use religion to get what they want and to take advantage of others. Jesus grew angry about such people—He even knocked over a few tables when confronted with this kind of behavior.

No doubt, we'll meet people like this often as we try to follow Christ. There will be difficult times ahead of us, even though they may not be any more or less difficult than what any generation before us has experienced. But what we can do is learn from other generations. We can pay attention to our teachers. As Paul advised, "Stick with what you learned and believed. . . .There's nothing like the written Word of God for showing you the way to salvation through faith in Christ Jesus" (verses 14–15 MSG).

God, lead me through difficult times with Your Word. Amen.

Delight in Mercy

Who is a God like you, who pardons sin and forgives the transgression of the remnant of his inheritance? You do not stay angry forever but delight to show mercy.
MICAH 7:18

Karen looked at her phone for the tenth time that morning. She picked it up, pushed the button to see the screen come to life, checked for new messages, and then put the phone down again.

It's only been one night, she reminded herself.

She felt her heart sink. They'd had such an awful fight the previous day. They had both dredged up long-past sins and mistakes, calling each other to account for things that had been dealt with and buried. Karen tried to replay the afternoon in her head, trying to figure out what had gone wrong. Who had said what first? There were so many things she couldn't remember. But some words had stung so badly, she knew she'd never forget them.

But could she forgive? Last night, she had vowed she wouldn't. Why should she? She felt justified. Those accusations were wrong and unfair. And the names she had been called! There was no reason for that. No reason at all. Why would she forgive anyone who had deliberately tried to hurt her feelings? Even *her*.

But as she tried to kindle the angry flames she had felt inside several hours before, she found that she didn't feel angry anymore. She was just sad. And hurt. And afraid.

What if I call her, but she won't answer? Karen imagined. She didn't think she could stand that. Far better not to call at all than to face that kind of rejection. No, she'd just have to wait it out.

As she waited, she flipped open her Bible. Her eyes fell on a verse from Micah 7: "For a son dishonors his father, a daughter rises up against her mother, a daughter-in-law against her mother-in-law—a man's enemies are the members of his own household" (verse 6).

You got that right, Micah.

But as she read further, she realized the verses were being spoken about the nation of Israel. This nation of rescued slaves, who had endured so much and been given so much by God, so often chose to turn away from Him. God deserved their praise and honor, yet they often gifted Him with bitterness and rebellion instead.

But God did not stay angry with His people forever. Instead, He took delight in—He actually enjoyed—showing mercy to them. He hurled all their wrongs into the depths of the sea. If God could do that with the Israelites, maybe she could do it too.

"Hello, honey? It's Mama. Can we talk?"

Lord, help me not to hold grudges but to delight in offering mercy and forgiveness. Amen.

In the Dark

"Lord," they answered, "we want our sight."
MATTHEW 20:33

. . . .

Sometimes, we just make things difficult. We are so wrapped up in our wrongheaded desires, we can't see straight. We hide behind lies. We cover up our ambitions. We put more distance between ourselves and the people we've already pushed away. We disobey God and then keep running from Him.

In Matthew 20, we see two sets of two men asking for different things. One set blindly asked for something they couldn't even handle. And one set openly begged for a gift of mercy that they very much wanted.

God is not blind. He sees our motives. He sees our needs. He knows exactly what we want before we even figure out the words to ask—before we even realize what we want. Even when we are smack-dab in the middle of our sin and trying to hide away from the God of the universe, He sees us and knows what's on our hearts.

Zebedee's sons, James and John, wanted more authority. They wanted to be something great in the kingdom of heaven. Apparently, they hadn't been listening all that well to Jesus' sermons. They didn't realize that to be great, they had to be willing to be small. They were blinded by pride and ambition, and they couldn't see what Jesus was trying to tell them—that to sit at His right and left meant they would have to drink from His cup—a cup full of suffering.

As Jesus and the disciples were leaving that area, two men who were physically blind heard that Jesus was passing by, and they shouted out to Him, with no shred of shame, "Lord, Son of David, have mercy on us!" (Matthew 20:30).

Jesus heard them—of course He did! "What do you want me to do for you?" (verse 32).

The men asked for their sight. That's all. They just wanted to be made well again—to be healed so they could look on the face of the Son of God. They had no ulterior motives (that we know of). They just wanted to see.

And Jesus, seeing their need, realized that these two men knew exactly what they were asking for, though they didn't know how it would change their lives. "Jesus had compassion on them and touched their eyes. Immediately they received their sight" (verse 34). But that wasn't the end of their story. They could have gone anywhere, done all sorts of things they hadn't been able to do before. What did they do when they could see again?

They followed Him.

Because when you finally can see, you don't want to waste any more time in the dark.

Lord, help me to see You clearly. Amen.

Speak Truth

*Therefore each of you must put off falsehood and speak truthfully
to your neighbor, for we are all members of one body.*
EPHESIANS 4:25

It would have been enough if Paul had put the period after "neighbor." Certainly, we all understand the command to speak truthfully to one another. We have known since we were small children that telling a fib is a bad thing. We know it's wrong to lie. We know it's wrong to carry around falsehood with us and wear it like a robe. Or do we?

Spending even a little time on social media sites is enough to see that wearing falsehood is the latest style. People put on fake smiles to go with their fake hair and fake makeup as they stand in front of the one cleaned-up corner of one fake room and pretend that their whole house looks just like that—giving off a vibe of casual yet elegant organization. People "get real" by revealing their somewhat colorful thoughts about one small aspect of life—but only such opinions that they feel absolutely certain will obtain a large number of "likes" from their eagerly waiting social media audience.

Let's be honest with each other here for a moment, friends. We aren't really all that honest, are we? We aren't really committed to putting off falsehood and wearing truth instead. But here's the reason we need to stop messing around and start getting good at it—today.

"We are all members of one body."

Think about it. What happens when you lie to yourself for a long time? Let's take one small lie—like lying to yourself that those extra thirty (or forty, fifty, sixty. . .) pounds you are carrying around really don't matter. You are just as healthy, even if the stupid scale says you are overweight. Sure, you haven't thought about exercise much lately (or this century), but you feel great—right? Until the doctor tells you your cholesterol is way too high and explains what that does to your vital organs.

You can't lie to yourself without experiencing negative consequences. Your mind and heart will get split into two, or you will become a walking display of falsehood, or you will get sick. Or you will hurt somebody else.

And that is the problem. If you believe we are all part of one body—we are all in this thing called life together—then you must realize that what you do, even in the privacy of your own home, matters. What you say to and about yourself matters. What you say to and about your neighbor matters.

Lord, help me to tell true stories about You through the way I live my life every day. Amen.

Count the Stars

"Look up at the sky and count the stars—if indeed you can count them." Then he said to him, "So shall your offspring be."
GENESIS 15:5

Abram must have been tired. He had just made it through a rather hard battle—fighting off four kings and their armies in order to rescue his nephew Lot. He must have been taking a moment to try to process it all. As night fell, he sat in his tent and wondered what God had in mind for him next.

He didn't have to wonder for long.

God answered Abram's questioning about his future, about his family. He brought Abram outside. Abram walked away from the campfire, away from the other tents. He stood under the vast night sky—the same piece of sky that one day Ruth would sleep under as she lay in the protection of her kinsman, Boaz. The same piece of sky that someday a boy named David would be singing under as he watched his sheep. The same piece of sky in which, one day far away, a new star would appear, shining down a path to the new Savior of the world.

God brought Abram out under this blanket of night filled with thousands upon thousands of pinpricks of light, and He said, "Count the stars." Abram raised his gray head and stared into the galaxy. Once again, God was asking him to do something impossible. *Have a baby when you're a hundred, Abram. Count the millions of stars, Abram.* Who did God think Abram was, anyway?

But God did know who Abram was. He was keenly aware of Abram's limitations, of his humanity. God was never asking Abram to do impossible things. He was never setting Abram up to fail. He was always asking Abram to do just one thing—trust Him. And Abram did. He believed God. He believed God's promises were true, and this was credited to Abram as righteousness (Genesis 15:6).

What impossible task has God set before you? Has He asked you to count the grains of salt in a shaker, or the number of times your children have said your name in the last twenty-four hours? In what ways has God been nudging you, asking you to trust Him more?

When night comes, go out and sit under the sky. Ask God where He is sending you. Talk to Him about His promises that you read in His Word. Then look up into the vast field of stars and start counting. And with every star, begin to trust God just a little bit more.

*Lord who formed the stars and set each one
into the sky, thank You for Your promises. Amen.*

Sinking Faith

But when he saw the strength of the wind, he was afraid,
and beginning to sink he cried out, "Lord, save me!"
MATTHEW 14:30 CSB

How simple it had seemed to Sam when he set out on his life's journey to be a pastor. How fervent was his faith in Jesus, fervent in the face of all worldly unbelief! His was a faith that could move mountains. He remembered the excitement he felt when he was in seminary. The future seemed so full of promise. But now these days he was living out seemed so far away from all that excitement and anticipation. Now there were bills to be paid, a family that was poorer than anything he had envisioned, and a flock to be ministered to. He had never considered the extreme efforts that he would have to make to keep body and soul together. The realities were truly awful when measured against his dreams.

But when he came to this passage one morning, he thought about Peter imploring the Lord in the night: "Lord, if it's you. . . command me to come to you on the water" (verse 28 CSB).

And he realized that Peter, Jesus' rock, had also experienced a time in his life when he thought his faith would carry him through, only to find himself sinking. He reflected that perhaps he was now having his "Peter moment"; he too had believed that his faith in Jesus would carry him against everything the world could bring to bear, would keep him from sinking into the waves and enable him to walk on water. And now, just like Peter, he was being overcome by the waves.

Then he took hold of the final three words Peter called out to Jesus: "Lord, save me." He saw that in the very moment Peter lost faith, he also recovered it. At the same time that he lost faith in his ability to walk on water, he turned to Jesus to keep him from sinking and drowning.

We too live in a world in which Jesus becomes harder and harder to see and recognize, like Jesus in the night on the sea. How often do the challenges of the world obscure the face of Jesus? And when we would make headway, when we think that we see Jesus—when we think that Jesus is calling us onto the water, and we set out with all confidence and faith—how often do we find ourselves quailing on the waters, frightened like Peter into thinking that sinking is a likelier bet than keeping our feet? "O ye of little faith," keep your eyes on Jesus. That is His will for us.

Lord, save me. Amen.

Watch and Pray

*"Watch and pray so that you will not fall into temptation.
The spirit is willing, but the flesh is weak."*
MATTHEW 26:41

Tired. That one word describes so many of us at so many points in our lives. For some of us, it's a daily state of being. And no matter what walk of life we come from, we can all understand this feeling. The mother of the newborn infant is tired. The late-night bus driver is tired. The high-powered CEO with a company in financial stress is tired. The cafeteria worker doling out dollops of mashed potatoes to loudmouthed elementary-school kids is tired. The teacher working two jobs is tired. The single dad trying to take care of his three young boys is tired. The refugee trying to sleep in a crowded tent is tired. The soldier standing guard is tired.

None of us is meant to live as a tired person day in and day out. When we are tired, we are in a weakened state. Often our brains don't function quite as well. Some studies have shown that driving tired is actually more dangerous than driving drunk. Our reflexes are sluggish when we are tired. Our thinking is clouded. Our feelings sometimes get out of control.

If you are tired, you may be tempted to do something you wouldn't otherwise want to do.

Jesus knew His friends were tired. It had already been a long, emotionally charged day. And here He was, their Savior and the Son of God, telling them that He would soon be betrayed and that He was going to have to die. The disciples were confused. They stayed close to Jesus, trying to make sense of it all and perhaps even trying to protect Him.

Jesus wanted to have some words alone with His Father. But He also cherished this time with His friends. Peter and James and John went with Jesus as He walked farther into the garden. They saw the shadow of sorrow pass over Jesus' face. Jesus asked them to stay and keep watch with Him as He went to pray.

But when He came back, He found that His friends had fallen asleep. It wasn't surprising. Jesus woke them up. "Watch and pray." Even in this moment of His great sorrow, Rabbi Jesus stopped to instruct His friends in a lesson for life. He indicated that prayer was a way to stay alert and not let ourselves fall, unwittingly or otherwise, into one of our temptations. Prayer can keep us on our toes, even when we are weary.

Are you tired? Are you struggling to stay close to Jesus? Watch and pray.

*Jesus, I ask You to help me be strong,
even when I have no strength left. Amen.*

Refuge

The LORD is a refuge for the oppressed,
a stronghold in times of trouble.
PSALM 9:9

We can look around us, through the lens of journalists and reporters, and see so many hurting people all around the world. So many thousands and thousands of people have had to flee their homes. So many have been waiting even years now for relief. So many seem not to have a voice. So many are fighting for justice. So many seem to be just struggling to survive.

But God promises us over and over again in scripture that He will "never forget the needy; the hope of the afflicted will never perish" (Psalm 9:18). The Bible is filled with stories of God rescuing those who were treated unfairly. From the Israelites being led out of slavery to the followers of Jesus being released from the bondage of sin through repentance and baptism, God has been saving people from the forces of darkness since darkness first entered the world.

God, the perfect Judge, "rules the world in righteousness and judges the peoples with equity" (verse 8). Some of this judgment we see come to pass, when corrupt men get arrested and tried for their crimes, or when victims receive restitution. But sometimes we don't get to see righteousness come about in ways that are obvious to us. In those times we have to trust that God's Word is still just as true and faithful. We have to believe in His promises. We have to remember all that He has done—all the good in the world we have already witnessed come about.

And we also can be a part of His goodness. We can be the hands and feet of Jesus, bringing relief to those who are suffering and hope to those who have been disappointed. We can bring love to those who need to be held. We can speak truth to those who are confused and wondering. We can give medicine and food and shelter to those who are in need. We can comfort those who are mourning. And we can remind every person that God sees them, God knows them by name, and He has "never forsaken those who seek [Him]" (verse 10).

And because God remembers them and knows them by name, we have to get to know them too, and never forget those who are in trouble, whether it's the family down the street who lost their home in a fire, or the family across the ocean who are trying to turn a rescue tent into a home.

Lord of the lonely and hurting and afraid, help me to be Your helper.
Help me to stand for justice. Help me to be a voice for the oppressed. Amen.

Goals

*For Jews request a sign, and Greeks seek after wisdom; but we preach Christ crucified,
to the Jews a stumbling block and to the Greeks foolishness, but to those who are called,
both Jews and Greeks, Christ the power of God and the wisdom of God.*

1 CORINTHIANS 1:22–24 NKJV

Macey had been working for a nonprofit organization for years. The organization helped many people, and the people she worked with were dedicated and hardworking. But lately she wasn't so sure about the purpose and the goal of her work. She knew the numbers of people they were assisting and where and who they were. All of that could be displayed on a spreadsheet. Every year there was a big meeting to recruit new workers and volunteers, letting the world know just how much the organization was doing to address the needs of the poor, the homeless, and the abandoned.

Yet Macey continued to experience a kind of personal malaise. After much reflection, she came to the conclusion that the problem had less to do with any material conditions and more to do with spiritual matters. She realized that when she had started out, her goals had much more to do with her relationship with Jesus, but with the passing of years, she had lost touch with her beginnings and most especially with her open line to Jesus. She had allowed herself to get caught up in the numbers for so long that the truly substantial things had fallen by the wayside.

One Friday, when Macey was having lunch with a colleague, she expressed her misgivings to him. Harold was a good guy, down-to-earth and honest, the sort of person who said what was on his mind and let the chips fall where they may. "It sounds to me like you need to get your eyes back on the prize," he counseled her nonchalantly.

"Now what is that supposed to mean?" she retorted. "It's the prize and prizes that are wearing me down as it is. Isn't there supposed to be something more?"

"Yeah," he shot back. "There is supposed to be something more, and there is something more. Just like Paul says. We don't look for signs or arguments or worldly victories; 'we preach Christ crucified.' "

"What's that supposed to mean?" she asked.

"It means that you're in it for love or you're not in it at all," he said. "That's what Jesus is about; that's the cross. The rest of it doesn't amount to a hill of beans. Keep your eye, your inner eye, fixed on the cross, on the love of God for the world, and you'll be okay."

Jesus, my Lord, remind me why I do what I do. Amen.

Consider Your Heart

"What's wrong?" they asked. "Do you come in peace?"
1 Samuel 16:4 nlt

Pastor Jim was a good man. His spirit exuded warmth and goodness. He made people feel good when he was around them. And he was not afraid to speak the truth.

It was that last thing that sometimes made people walk the other way when they saw Pastor Jim coming. People who were struggling to do right, who were battling temptation, who were knowingly giving in to their desires—these people tended to disappear when Pastor Jim came around.

This avoidance frustrated the good man—it wasn't as if he didn't know what was going on. He was a godly man, not a gullible one. Though he never participated in the spreading of rumors, it was easy to pick up on the latest news (it was a small town and a small congregation).

Besides that, he prayed daily for God to open his eyes to the needs of those around him. And God often did. Jim could see when people were wrestling with spiritual problems. He wanted to tell these poor souls that they weren't fooling anyone—and they certainly weren't fooling God. Mostly, he wanted to tell people that God didn't care that they felt ashamed or embarrassed or unworthy—that God still wanted to love them anyway, no matter what kind of mess they'd entangled themselves in. He wanted to tell them that God knew their hearts.

Like Jim, Samuel was a good man, a prophet of the Lord. He tried to do what God told him to do. And he was an adviser to the king of Israel. Because of his position before God, people were a little skittish when they saw Samuel coming. After all, when Samuel opened his mouth, sometimes God's words would come out. And God's words to His people often were not complimentary.

It's no wonder then that the elders of Bethlehem came with trembling to meet Samuel. What was he going to say? What had they done wrong? But Samuel had come to anoint a king for God. He had come to anoint, in fact, the king who would stand in the line of the King of kings and Lord of lords.

As the prophet looked at the sons of Jesse, God reminded Samuel not to judge as people often did—by appearances. "People judge by outward appearance, but the Lord looks at the heart" (1 Samuel 16:7 nlt).

How does your heart look today? Would you come trembling before Samuel, or would you walk the other way? If you've been avoiding godly truth, consider your heart. But for goodness' sake, come to God anyway.

Lord, examine my heart. Instruct me in Your way. Amen.

Be Known

"Believe me, I don't know you!"
MATTHEW 25:12 NLT

Mary Pat was a very popular student at her college. She was an outstanding freshman athlete who played volleyball. She was a strong student also, and quite pretty. As a result, she had a lot of friends and hardly ever spent much time alone. That was good, because she didn't like being by herself. In fact, she flitted around from friend to friend and hardly really knew anyone, and no one really knew her. One weekend, her friend Eileen invited Mary Pat to her church, and while she thought attending church was sort of a corny thing to do, she agreed. She liked Eileen, and it was something to do.

Off to church they went. At church the minister preached about the ten virgins, and he focused on what the Lord had to say to the unprepared virgins when they finally arrived at the door with their lamps and asked to be let in: "Believe me, I don't know you!" He talked about people who lived by themselves, solitary, lonely, and relatively unknown, and the sadness of those lives but for Jesus. He discussed how no one wants to live and die unknown to anyone, and that fact was evidenced in the punishment of the virgins. The Lord said simply, "I do not know you." Mary Pat was surprised by what the minister was saying—struck by it, actually flustered by it, she realized.

As they were making their way back to campus, she asked Eileen, "Do you have any really close friends?"

"Well, I don't have close friends here at school yet, but at home I have two real soul mates," she replied. "You know, the kind of friends who know what you're going to say before you say it." Then she said, "You may think this is silly, but I like to think that God knows me too. That's why I go to church and pray." She blushed a little and shrugged her shoulders. "Maybe that's too much information."

"No, it's not," Mary Pat said. "I'm just realizing for the first time that while I don't live a lonely life, I don't have anyone who really knows me, here or at home. And except for when I need a really good grade or something like that, I hardly ever pray. So I can't really say that I have a friend in God either."

"Well, there's still plenty of time to take care of that," Eileen said, smiling and holding the door open to the campus café. "But right now, how about some brunch?"

Are you keeping the door open for God to know you?

Lord, I want to know You and be known by You. Amen.

Eyes Up

*I lift up my eyes to the mountains—
where does my help come from?*
PSALM 121:1

Look up. What do you see? Put down the book. Put down your phone. Put down your schedule. Put down your fears. Put down your stress. Put down the to-do list. Put down all the distractions and temptations and self-recriminations.

Look up. Eyes up, neck bent back, shoulders relaxed, fingers stretching toward the ground, mouth wide open—breathe deeply. What do you see?

Maybe you see a blank ceiling. A clean space. A space with no mistakes in it. Imagine the Creator God beginning to paint on this blank canvas. And with each stroke, a new part of creation appears. A lion leaps out on the plains of Africa. A whale bursts through the surface of the blue ocean. What do you see? Watch the Maker of heaven and earth at work. What do you notice about the colors and the textures and the details that He creates? What can you tell from the care He takes with every stroke?

Maybe you look up into the blue expanse above. What do you see? Is the sun shining? What do you hear? Look at every cloud, every leaf, every squirrel, every feather. What surprises you? What can you hear now that you couldn't before? Take time to look and listen. Look for the Creator's hand; listen for the Maker's commands. He who once said, "Let there be light," is now speaking something into being in your life: "Let there be. . ." What is it that you are welcoming into your life from the Maker's hands? What is it you are trying to push away? Breathe in the air and realize there is space in you for whatever God has for you to do. He designed that space. He has known about it all along. He has been preparing good works for you to do.

Maybe you look up and see the night sky. Reach up. Let your fingers play among the stars. Imagine reaching higher and higher. Reach up to your Maker and don't be afraid. He will not let you slip. All through the night, He will hang on to you. He will not slumber. He will not fall asleep on the job. He will watch over you all through this night, and all through any darkness you have to travel. He will bring you out of that blackness with the light of the sun or the light of the moon, or even with the Light of His Son. He will watch you come and go, come and go, today and tomorrow and forever.

Maker and Helper, thank You for watching over me. Amen.

Life and Peace

For to be carnally minded is death,
but to be spiritually minded is life and peace.
ROMANS 8:6 NKJV

Children, especially quite young ones, are carnal little beings. They are driven by their physical desires. They are hungry and cry out and have tantrums and yell and fuss. They get sleepy and nod their heads and bump into things and cry out and have tantrums and yell and fuss. They are uncomfortable—too hot, too cold, too wet, too dry—and they steal comforts from other children and cry out and have tantrums and yell and fuss.

Are you getting the picture? When we are very small, we have a proportional amount of control over our actions. We cannot understand the connections between our physical desires and our own behavior. We just want what we want when we want it. We can't see past the moment. We can't even see past the room we are standing in.

As grown people shepherding little ones, we are aware of their limitations. We know they have to be watched because their desires can lead them into danger. A desire to grab a treat can end up with a glass being broken. A desire for sleep can end up with them falling down on the ground in the path of an unsuspecting bicycling child. A desire to receive comfort or to express displeasure can lead them to run right out of the house and into a busy street.

Though our desires may become more sophisticated as we grow older, the connection to danger is no less strong. Feeding our physical desires alone, with no thought for the consequences and no attention to our spiritual growth, will lead us to death. If being carnally minded does not lead us to a physical death, it will be a spiritual one—our souls will become trapped by our own bad choices and we'll be launched into a cycle of desire and decay and destruction that can be hard to break.

But we have been freed from this cycle by Christ Jesus, who came to earth in the flesh to know us, to walk alongside us, and to help us gain victory over the desires of the flesh, and a final victory over death. "For those who live according to the flesh set their minds on the things of the flesh, but those who live according to the Spirit, the things of the Spirit" (Romans 8:5 NKJV).

Now that we are free, let us practice that freedom by focusing our minds on the Spirit living within us, and listening to His leading.

God, bring peace to my life by helping me
focus on what is most important. Amen.

Pretenders

*You are following a different way that pretends to
be the Good News but is not the Good News at all.*
GALATIANS 1:6–7 NLT

Now, perhaps more than ever, we are living in a time when it is hard to figure out who is a trustworthy source. Some people say follow this person. Others say you can trust that person. We can do some research and find some answers, but not all, and then it's hard to trust the source of those answers.

But does that mean we should give up trying? Should we just shrug our shoulders and say it's impossible to trust anyone? Should we just blindly follow whoever has the strongest voice? Should we stop seeking the truth?

Surely the answer to these questions is no. We are called as children of God to be seekers of the Truth and to be speakers of the truth. How do we do that?

The best way is to start and end with the Word of God. If we hear someone claiming to preach the Gospel of Jesus, it's not hard to compare their words to the story of Jesus in the Bible. Even in matters that are more flexible to interpretation, we can look in God's Word and see if all the threads of the message line up with the statements of Jesus and with the story of God's people.

For instance, if a speaker claims to be preaching the Gospel of Christ, and yet they leave out the need for people to come to repentance, we can look in God's Word and clearly find repentance being preached. We can conclude that the speaker either is not a reliable source for wisdom or has made a grave oversight in preaching the Word of God.

Or if a speaker claims to be preaching the Good News but then talks about the resurrection of Jesus as only a symbol and not a reality, we can go to God's Word and contrast its truth with the message we heard.

Or if a speaker claims to be telling us about anything—how to love others, how to know God's will, how to receive Jesus' salvation—and yet that speaker lives in a way that is contrary to everything that is spoken, we can go to God's Word and see the inconsistencies being presented and conclude that the speaker does not seem to know the truth of Jesus.

We should not condemn any speaker, however. We are not the distributors of condemnation and judgment—God will do the judging. But we can and should be discerning seekers of the truth.

*God of the Good News, help me to be a truthful
speaker of that Good News to everyone I see. Amen.*

Mixed Emotions

Even in laughter the heart may ache,
and rejoicing may end in grief.
PROVERBS 14:13

· ·

What a confusing place is the human heart! One minute we are in love, and the next we are bitterly angry. At one turn we are happy and whole, and around another corner come distress and emptiness. We are lonely; we are suffocated by other souls. We are afraid; we are taking risks. We are desperately longing for love and care; we are rejecting friends and shutting down.

The human heart is changeable and even at times deceitful. It can fool us into thinking things that are not so—into seeing mountains where there is only mist.

And when we are journeying through grief, we may find it hard to understand the sea of feelings we must swim through day after day. At one moment we might find satisfaction and contentment in knowing our loved ones have gone (or are going) to live eternally with God. In the next moment we may feel angry about being left on earth alone. One day we may feel too weary to cry another drop. And then in another hour a silly commercial jingle can trigger a memory that leaves us reeling with huge, shuddering sobs.

The feelings of grief can surprise us. They can leap upon us without notice, being conjured up from a glimpse of a house through a car window, from the sight of a picture on a wall, or from the vision of our loved ones visiting us in our dreams. These heavy feelings can rest on our shoulders when we hear a particular saying or the chorus of a familiar song. These feelings can stop us in our tracks when someone asks a simple question such as "How's your dad doing?"

One of the hardest things about traveling through grief is feeling that there is some sort of right way to do it. We sometimes think there's a correct way to grieve, and if our feelings don't line up with that way, we must be doing it wrong. But there is no standard road map through grief. Everyone's trip is different, even though some of the signs along the way are familiar.

The writer of this proverb understood this truth. There is wisdom in knowing that some things are just inexplicable. There is no reason for the mysterious ability to laugh even when our hearts are aching. There is no logic to a moment of rejoicing turning into an expression of sorrow. But the God who made us knows all the mysterious revolutions of the human heart, and He will help us navigate the journey of grief.

♥ · ♥ · ♥ · ♥ ·

God of sorrows, You understand my pain
better than anyone. Please help me. Amen.

All Things

For from him and through
him and for him are all things.
ROMANS 11:36

. . . .

"Oh, the depth of the riches of the wisdom and knowledge of God!" (Romans 11:33).

Just consider the range of subjects that our God and Father understands. Nothing is beyond His comprehension. Nothing is below His consideration. Even our smallest needs and the flitting thoughts of our distracted brains are known to Him. There is nothing that we should feel is too trivial to bring to Him. We can talk with Him about anything we feel, anything we see, anything we hear. We can talk with Him about controversies and complicated relationships. We can talk with Him about problems that we can't seem to wrap our heads around.

"How unsearchable his judgments, and his paths beyond tracing out!" (verse 33).

God is the only perfect judge in the world. We are warned not to judge others—not just because we don't have the mind of God, but because when we place ourselves in the seat of judgment, we put ourselves at risk of also being judged. But even worse than that, what we really put at risk is the ability to have real relationships with people. It's easy to put people in boxes and slap on labels. It's difficult to have actual conversations with people and get to know their stories.

We will never be able to understand all the judgments of God. The paths that lead to where He sits are not known to us—we cannot see from His point of view. But we can be assured that what God is doing is for our good.

"Who has known the mind of the Lord? Or who has been his counselor?" (verse 34).

How good it is to know that no one on earth or in the heavenly realms understands the infinite mind of God! Our God is limitless. Our God is beyond definitions. Our God is bigger, grander, deeper than anything we could ever hope to imagine. And yet He wants us—smaller, lesser, shallower—to be with Him.

" 'Who has ever given to God, that God should repay them?' For from him and through him and for him are all things" (verses 35–36).

God does not need our gifts. God does not need anything. But we need to give to Him. We need to be placed in that position of gratitude—to practice offering up something of ourselves for something that is bigger than us. We need to practice letting go of our things and to be reminded that we are more than the things we own.

"To him be the glory forever! Amen" (verse 36).

Lord, all glory and honor belong to You. Amen.

Look at the Birds

"Look at the birds of the air; they do not sow or reap or store away in barns, and yet your heavenly Father feeds them."
MATTHEW 6:26

When Sally and Jason were planning their wedding, Jason chose this passage from Matthew 6: "Look at the birds of the air; they do not sow or reap or store away in barns, and yet your heavenly Father feeds them." While Sally liked the reading well enough, she found it confusing in a way. Was Jesus encouraging people not to be responsible? What did it mean for Him to suggest that people use the birds as their model? She didn't understand, so she asked Jason what he liked about the verse and how he understood it.

At first he stumbled around, trying to get a fix on his thoughts, but then something occurred to him that enabled him to explain what he had on his mind and in his heart. He recounted this story: "I knew a guy once, a young guy around my age, who had lost his job and was unemployed for about nine months. And as time went on in his search for work, he began to struggle—behind in rent, fearful of eviction, not eating so well, and so on. And there was no family to fall back on—nothing there. But he did go to church. And finally, he did get work. And he told me that he felt relief when he was working again, not so much because of the job, but because he had realized during his trials that he really did have faith. He said that after a while, he would pray to God for anything—not just for a job, but for a handout, or to find money on the street, a dropped scratch-off ticket—anything. 'And anything I got,' he said, 'I was grateful for. Even if I was hungry a lot, I was alive, and God was coming through for me.'

"When I think about that passage from Matthew," Jason explained, "sooner or later, I think of him—a man who became for a time like one of the birds in the sky that Jesus talks about. In his need and in his prayers, he had a faith-filled insight: Please, God, take care of me any way You see fit. I don't think his pastor ever had to plead too urgently with him about serving God rather than the world." Sally mentioned that it was hard to have that kind of faith, and Jason nodded. But they both agreed it was a good thing to shoot for as they started out in wedded life.

Please, God, take care of me any way You see fit. Amen.

Treasures of Restlessness

"I have no rest;
only trouble comes."
JOB 3:26 NLT

Sometimes we need to be shaken. It's true. Life gets far too easy and we get way too comfortable sitting down in our circumstances. We get so comfy, we forget why we're here. We lose track of days and years and forget all about going out and loving others and telling them about the love of Christ. We get so busy just living in the day-to-day that we forget about the eternal tomorrow that is waiting for us. We forget all about really following God's Word and doing His work and learning how to be who He created us to be.

It's not that we should go looking for suffering on purpose. No one needs to do that. We should not be pain seekers. But when trials come, we need to remember that being troubled by troubles is perfectly normal and even a good thing. Being troubled shows us that we are familiar with peace. Being troubled shows us that we do have good things in our lives and reasons to be thankful. Being troubled reminds us who is really in control.

Job was a man in trouble. Extreme trouble. He'd had almost everything he cared about stripped from him—his family members, his property, even his own health. And in his suffering and pain, he wished he had never been born. His worst fears had come true. He had no peace and no quiet. Only trouble. (See Job 3:25–26.)

But through these trials, and through the added burden of having to endure the well-meaning but misguided words of friends, Job met God in a way he never had before. He said, "I had only heard about you before, but now I have seen you with my own eyes. I take back everything I said, and I sit in dust and ashes to show my repentance" (Job 42:5–6 NLT).

Job learned about who God is, but he also learned about himself. He learned that the bottom line to every experience we will ever have is that God is in charge. Only God. He's the only Author of our lives. He's our Creator and our King. And He is good. No matter what we think or do or say, no matter what power we think we might have, no matter how well we think we've got everything figured out, the only One who really understands the big picture is God.

Sometimes we need to be made restless before we can find true rest. Sometimes we need to be brought down low so we can know where to look for help.

You, oh Lord, are everything to me.
Help me remember who You are. Amen.

King of the Flood

*The L*ORD *sits enthroned over the flood; the L*ORD *is enthroned as King forever.*
*The L*ORD *gives strength to his people; the L*ORD *blesses his people with peace.*
PSALM 29:10–11

. . . .

Drip. Drop. That's how it started—just a sprinkle. Then the sprinkle turned into a steady rain. Then torrents of rain beat down on the community. The creeks spilled over. The rivers burst out of their banks. And the water kept coming.

There is little peace when the floodwaters are rising, the rain is still pouring, and your front steps are just feet away from trouble. Little peace, and yet so little you can actually do. You can't stop the rain. You can't hem in the rivers. You can't build a wall to keep the waters out of your house.

All you really can do is pray.

Floods are one kind of trouble. But often our troubles come in floods. The old saying "When it rains, it pours" rings true more regularly than we'd like. And in those times when the accidents and mistakes and bad luck and disappointments pile up one on top of another like some giant totem pole of misfortune, it's easy to feel forgotten. It's easy to believe God has left the building. Maybe He's on vacation, or just busy with another mess somewhere else in the world. Or maybe He's just mad at us.

But when torrents of trouble come, the best thing we can do is take shelter under the One who "sits enthroned over the flood" (Psalm 29:10). Because no matter how we feel about the situation, no matter how helpless we are, and no matter where we think God may have gone off to, the fact remains that He is the best person in our lives to help us.

People may try to help. And we definitely should try to lift one another up. We especially should protect the weaker ones among us and look out for those who are alone or abandoned. But we cannot depend on humans to give us everything we need. And when those floodwaters of strife begin to recede, the real work of healing and cleaning and rebuilding begins.

Our Lord is mighty and powerful. He can give us strength. He can reach into our hearts and mend our wounds. He can see into our minds and help us untangle the knots we get ourselves tied up in through poor decisions or negative patterns.

God will not always stop the floods from coming. But He will always be with us in the water.

God of the flood of my troubles, wash over me. Let my stress
and my pain bring me humbly to the shore of Your peace. Amen.

Anguish

*"I have been praying here out
of my great anguish and grief."*
1 Samuel 1:16

She looked down at the plate of food in front of her and felt the acid rising up in her throat, touching the back of her tongue. Her stomach ached with hunger, but she could not bring herself to eat. Salty tears dropped down onto the food—a preservative of grief.

She wasn't sure how much longer she could live like this. It was bad enough to feel so useless. It was hard enough to feel this endless longing deep within her. It was painful enough to have her hopes dashed time after time when her womb remained empty. But to have this woman in her life, poking at her pain, ridiculing her, reminding her every day of what she lacked, of how clearly she was deficient—Hannah just couldn't take it anymore.

She pushed away the plate that her husband had generously filled—giving her more than anyone else. She appreciated his tenderness toward her, but she could not stand to look into his eyes and see his pity growing. She did not want to be pitied. She wanted to be strong.

Hannah felt the tears filling her eyes and swallowed down sobs as she made her way to the house of the Lord. She dropped to her knees at the doorway and let the emptiness fill her up and spill out onto the ground. Through her sobs, she made this silent vow to God: if He would give her a son, she would give Him a servant.

Eli the priest was sitting nearby, watching Hannah, confused by her behavior. She seemed so out of control that at first he thought this woman must be drunk. But Hannah explained, "I am a woman who is deeply troubled" (1 Samuel 1:15).

Eli then recognized the anguish in the woman's face. He had seen this brand of pain before. "Go in peace," he said, "and may the God of Israel grant you what you have asked of him" (verse 17).

Hannah felt some weight lifted off her heart. She had done all she could do. She had made a true promise to God. Now she just had to trust Him. And she did.

The Lord remembered Hannah. And in time, she had a son. But God remembers every woman suffering, with silent words of anguish on her lips. Not every woman will have a baby, but God will give each one exactly what she needs. We just have to keep trusting Him.

*You are the God who hears me
and sees me. I will trust You. Amen.*

Free Me

*Who will free me from this life
that is dominated by sin and death?*
ROMANS 7:24 NLT

. . . .

You know you've felt it. You've been sitting at that traffic light, waiting for the green and staring out at the horizon. And the thought has gone through your head, *What if I just kept going? What if I just kept driving straight ahead. . .out of town, out of the state, all the way to the ocean? What then?*

We all want to escape our lives sometimes. Usually, when the mountain of life's details feels too heavy to manage, or when bigger troubles are sitting like stubborn storm clouds over our households, or when we're so stressed and exhausted we can't even define what's bothering us, that's when the escape plan seems particularly attractive. And it's never that we want to leave our loved ones behind. We don't really want to shake up our entire lives. We just want a break. Really, we just want a vacation from being. . .us.

Paul understood this feeling. He had felt frustrated and confused by his own jumbled mixture of motivations, intentions, and actions. "I don't really understand myself, for I want to do what is right, but I don't do it. Instead, I do what I hate" (Romans 7:15 NLT). He recognized the strength of the sinful nature within him—how it kept blocking him from his desires to do good.

The power of this sinful nature is what makes us feel so trapped in our lives. It's not that anything happening around us is overwhelming. When we sit down and put it all on paper, we can see what's right to do. We can find at least a few potential solutions to our complex problems. Often our troubles are not at all the things that are happening outside of us. It's the trouble inside that keeps us tied in knots. And we can't escape ourselves.

Being a slave to our sinful nature keeps us from enjoying all the good gifts God wants us to have. But thanks be to God, He can free us. *How do I get free from myself? How do I break the cycle of sin and shame?* The answer is always Jesus. We can't do it on our own. We can't even do it together. And we can't do it just by obeying a set of laws. We have to have Jesus.

"Because you belong to him, the power of the life-giving Spirit has freed you from the power of sin that leads to death" (Romans 8:2 NLT). The next time you are sitting at that light, waiting for go, don't dream about getting away. Dream about getting closer to God.

Lord, free me from the hold of sin. Amen.

Waves

Deep calls to deep in the roar of your waterfalls;
all your waves and breakers have swept over me.
PSALM 42:7

Crashing, falling, rushing. Enormous power channeled into curves and curls moves rapidly down the river, hurrying to the edge of the land as if an important appointment is waiting on the other side. The water leaps out and then falls forcefully into the pool below—a faucet that is never shut off.

Grief is like that sometimes. It seems like it will never end. Just when you feel you are over it, another wave comes, welling up inside you until it feels like your chest will explode with the pressure. Some days it grabs you all of a sudden—a memory rises up in your mind and you see the familiar scene play out like a movie. You watch the characters interact, you hear their lines, and you see them play their roles, but then comes the devastating realization that you will never be able to live that scene again. You'll never be able to hear that voice. You'll never be able to touch that hand.

And there you are, in the grip of grief. Air sucked out of your lungs. Mind swept of whatever thing you were supposed to be focusing on. Body frozen as you struggle to keep the tears from falling.

Grief lives deep inside you—underneath all the day-to-day activities that you use to try to stay busy. You put one foot in front of another and keep walking, but grief makes each step a little heavier. It's like the beat of a song that no one wants to sing. It's the experience of your heart breaking again and again. Grief is exhausting.

And down in the depths of your weary sorrow, God is there, calling to you, deep to deep. By day, as you work and try to think a clear path through the fog, He directs His love toward you, surrounding you with comfort. At night, God sings over you, like a mother singing a lullaby to her frightened child. God reminds you that you are never ever alone.

And with that promise, hope comes. And with hope, healing. And eventually, someday, you'll be able to have the memories without the mourning. You'll be able to replay those scenes and rejoice in the love you were blessed to have.

Lord, I put my hope in You. I trust that You are preparing a
place where all of us can live and love together with You. Amen.

One Another

"By this everyone will know that you are my disciples, if you love one another."
JOHN 13:35

. . . .

Jena works in an executive-level corporate position around sixty hours each week. Her high salary is equivalent to the high amount of stress she experiences every month. A lot is riding on her abilities, and the decisions she makes affect many people. But on every Wednesday night, she's just one of the many faces behind the serving counters at the city soup kitchen. She loves being there and often calls it the highlight of her week. As busy as she is, she makes it her priority to serve. "Not because they need me," she says, "but because I need to be there. I need to remember that I'm part of a big family of all different kinds of people with all different kinds of struggles."

Kellie stays at home with her two children, ages three and seven. Her oldest has just started reading on her own. Kellie loves that she gets to teach her kids, but she finds herself feeling quite isolated at times. She wishes she knew other moms in the area, but her family just moved, and it's hard to get out to meet people. Some days she finds herself spending hours on social media pages. Some of the headline stories shock her and make her want to protect her children even more from the horrible world outside. She gets caught up in negative comments online and starts to worry. Her anxiety is increasing, and she keeps forgetting to pray about it, even though she encourages her kids to pray every day. Kellie realizes she needs to get out in her community to serve others. She sees an ad on Facebook for volunteers needed at the city soup kitchen. She hears God telling her that volunteering will both ease her anxious thoughts and give her the chance to break out of her isolation.

Lacey never dreamed that, at age forty-two, she'd be living on the streets. But a medical condition with expensive treatments put her behind on her rent. After a while, she was behind on everything, and her physical pain left her too exhausted to try to figure out the maze of government assistance programs. It just seemed easier to stay in the park where she liked to take walks every day. She got to know the other people living outside and organized group meetings where they would share tips for survival, play chess, or read books together. They often ate at the city soup kitchen together, and on Wednesday nights, Lacey always made sure to find Jena and ask her, "How's your heart, boss lady?"

And Jena always answered, "Better now, Miss Lacey!"

Jesus commanded us to love one another—not just because the others need love, but because we need to love others. We need to take our minds off ourselves and practice what it means to love. Every day.

Lord, help me to love like You. Amen.

Hiding Places

You are my hiding place;
you protect me from trouble.
PSALM 32:7 CSB

"Eighteen. . .nineteen. . .twenty! Ready or not, here I come!" And off he runs, searching for his hidden friends. The friends wait in eager anticipation, ready to spring out from behind trees and bushes to make a dash for home base. Because as much fun as it is to hide, it's still more fun to be found. To come out in the open and join the crowd and compare notes on who had the best hiding place, who was found first, and so on. The real fun of the game only happens in community. You can't play hide-and-seek alone.

It is a blessing to be out in the open and free—to feel as though you can be yourself without having to cover up any blemishes or faults. To feel that whatever wrong things you have done have been revealed and forgiven and can now be put behind you. To know you have learned and grown and changed and can now hope for better days.

The psalmist spoke of the damaging effects of hidden sin: "When I kept silent, my bones became brittle from my groaning all day long. . . . My strength was drained as in the summer's heat" (Psalm 32:3–4 CSB). Once our sin is confessed and forgiven, we can stop hiding away from God and instead turn and hide within God's protection—safe from trouble.

Hiding there with God, we can be protected by knowledge. God teaches us and provides wise counsel, showing the way we need to go to become the people He created us to be. With God, we can be surrounded by love—by the love of God that never fails and never fades, that doesn't require us to pretend to be anything different from what we are, but rather calls us to be honest and true. With God, we can be encouraged and lifted up by the joy of the Lord—and by the feeling of standing upright before Him!

God doesn't expect us to always make right choices. After all, He made us, and He has observed human behavior since the beginning. God is not surprised when we fail. So why hide? Come out, come out, wherever you are, and share your story. You'll be glad you did, and you'll help those who are listening to share their stories too.

Most holy God, please forgive all the ungodly parts of me.
I place myself in Your care. Hide me in Your love. Amen.

Better

*"Mary has chosen what is better,
and it will not be taken away from her."*
LUKE 10:42

She had started off well. Offering hospitality like a champ, Martha had welcomed in the unexpected visitors. But then. . .there was a meal to be made, and floors to clean, and furniture to move, and drinks to be fetched, and. . .what was that smell?

Martha just couldn't be still. There were so many things to be done. And if she didn't do them, who would?

She looked over at her sister, Mary. *Not her, that's for sure*, Martha thought. From the moment Jesus had entered the house, Mary hadn't left His side. She hung on His every word. We can imagine that Martha had tried in vain to get her sister's attention. Maybe she had cleared her throat loudly and lifted her eyebrows so severely that she almost frightened them right off her forehead. She might have tried staring her sister down with a glare that spoke volumes—at least a few choice paragraphs. She even might have crept up close to give Mary a loving nudge in the side. But it was no use. Mary wasn't budging.

Finally, the exasperated Martha just couldn't take it. Can't you just picture her in your mind? Coming away from the cooking fire, sweat dripping, hair curling around her neck, stains on her best dress—having lost her patience and her temper and her composure, she marched up to the Rabbi: "Lord, don't You care?" One wonders how she had finished that question in her head. *Don't You care at all that I'm doing all these things for You? Don't You care about how much work this is for me? Don't You care about me too, Lord? You haven't even asked what's for dinner! Don't You care?*

But what she said was, "Don't you care that my sister has left me to do the work by myself? Tell her to help me!" (Luke 10:40). It must be said: Martha had guts.

Ever full of grace, Jesus quieted Martha's worries. He took Martha's cares and distilled them down into what was important. He heard her, but He also knew what she needed to hear. She needed to know she was wrong. "Mary has chosen what is better, and it will not be taken away from her" (verse 42).

It was better to listen. It was better to be near Jesus. It was better not to be so caught up in the things of this world that she missed the presence of God. Right there in her own living room. What are you doing that's keeping you from the better choice?

Lord, don't let me forget that what matters most is You. Amen.

In All Things

And we know that in all things God works for the good of those
who love him, who have been called according to his purpose.
ROMANS 8:28

In all things. We tend to apply that phrase to, quite literally, all things. We say God is working for good when it's raining and we show up for that big presentation sopping wet and with mascara running, only to find that some extra-special visitors will unexpectedly be attending the meeting today—including the CEO and chairman of the board.

In all things. When we are trying to impress our children while at the same time trying to make ourselves feel a little younger, and we hop on that skateboard for all of two minutes before we fall and break an elbow, we say surely we can figure out how God is working for good in this experience. Like maybe how it allowed you to get to know the emergency nurses or how you'll be spending more time with your children since they will have to help with all the chores—is that how God is working for good in this thing?

In all things. Sometimes we struggle to find God in all things. When a child is murdered by a relative and through some fluke of the court system that person goes free, we find it hard to see God working in all things.

When a community that was already recently ravaged by flooding now experiences a horrific tornado that takes many lives, we try hard to find God in anything.

But the passage never promises we'll see God working. In fact, if you read the verses leading up to this bit, you'll see that the exact opposite is stated. Paul speaks to the Romans about a hope we cannot see, a time that creation itself has been waiting for, when the children of God will be revealed, and when the glory of God will be revealed. Paul clearly states that we don't have this vision yet, but we are waiting for it: "Hope that is seen is no hope at all" (Romans 8:24).

We don't even know what we ought to pray for sometimes—that's how clueless we are. We look around at this world and can't figure out where to start. But God knows. The Spirit prays for us—taking what's in our hearts and minds and weaving it together into a wordless whisper of longing and hope to God.

Yes, we can know—we can be sure—that the God who is perfectly good is working for the good of those who love Him. But we won't always be able to see it. And that's okay.

Lord, help me to be certain of You, even when I can't see. Amen.

Salty

*"You are the salt of the earth. But if the salt loses
its saltiness, how can it be made salty again?"*
MATTHEW 5:13

Have you ever had to be on a low-salt diet? It's hard to do. Really hard. Salt is in everything. Even things you never would have thought about. Even things that don't taste remotely salty.

In the days before refrigeration, salt was often used as a preservative. Salt sucks the water right out of foods. When the water is gone, so is the happy environment for bacteria and mold, and thus the food is kept edible for a longer time than it normally would be.

Salt was sometimes used as a way of holding on to heat, as part of road surfacing material, in cleaning, as part of roofing material, and the list goes on and on. Several reports claim that there are more than fourteen thousand uses for salt. But as useful as it is, once salt has lost its ability to function, or once it has lost its flavor, it is no longer any good to be used as salt. It becomes just another bit of dirt. It becomes something other than what it was meant to be.

We who follow Christ have certain jobs to do. We are gifted by the Spirit and called by Christ to act in certain ways and to perform specific acts of goodness and kindness and faithfulness. We are to live lives that look different from the lives of those around us. We are to be pure and peaceful, to be merciful and meek, to be righteous and poor in spirit, to mourn with those who mourn and rejoice with those who rejoice, and to keep on going and doing and being no matter what happens, or who hates us, or what is said about us because we love and serve Jesus.

If we lose our ability to be "salty"—to challenge people to enhance their lives with the Gospel and to preserve all that is good about the world—then we will have lost something of what it means to be a follower of Christ. We won't be the people God created us to be. But you don't have to be the most charismatic evangelist in the world; you don't have to be the most dynamic preacher; you don't have to be the wisest counselor in order to help people come to know Jesus. All you have to be is a little salty—be full of the Gospel, be truthful, be eager to show love and to serve others, and be well practiced in showing compassion. Be salty

*Jesus, help me to keep flavoring the lives of those
around me with the goodness of Your love. Amen.*

The Price of Forgiveness

*"But God sent me ahead of you to preserve for you a remnant
on earth and to save your lives by a great deliverance."*
GENESIS 45:7

If you didn't know the whole story, he would seem pretty cruel. Joseph, once a prisoner and slave, now second-in-command to Pharaoh, put his brothers through some psychological torture when they came to him seeking food. His brothers, those same men who at one time had contemplated killing him, didn't recognize Joseph. They weren't looking for him. Last time they saw him, he was sitting on the back of an Ishmaelite merchant wagon—sold as a slave.

Now he stood before them, full of power and holding the strings to their survival. And he seemed to be playing them like a puppet master with his marionettes. He gave them tasks to do, but he set them up to fail. He gave an appearance of being threatening, even when they had no knowledge of what they had done wrong.

Was he bitter? Vengeful? Just off his head?

None of those seem to be adequate explanations given what happened next—when Joseph could no longer hold in his emotions. It seems what was really running through Joseph's mind that whole time, his real feelings on seeing his family after so many years of being forgotten by them, was just. . .love.

It seems likely that Joseph all along was just trying to get all of his brothers together in one place and to get them used to being around him. Perhaps he wanted them to see and realize what power he had—not to lord it over them, but so he could later assure them that they were safe with him.

Of course, Joseph had every right to hold a grudge. No one would have been surprised if Joseph had wanted to exact some kind of revenge on his brothers. No one would have been shocked at all if he at least had been angry with them. But Joseph just wanted his family back. He gave up on retribution in order to have reconciliation. He gave up on punishment in order to have fellowship. He gave up personal pride in order to rejoice in family pride.

We sometimes have to let go of our own dreams about how things should be or what ought to be said in order to be open to the possibility of restored relationships. Forgiveness often costs us something. But the rewards are worth every penny.

*Lord, help me to let go of what I think is due
me and to accept all You have for me. Amen.*

Not Comparable

*For I consider that the sufferings of this present time are not
worth comparing with the glory that is going to be revealed to us.*
ROMANS 8:18 CSB

. . . .

"I remember thinking I was so miserable," the woman said, smiling. "Can you imagine? Misery? Over what? So my kids weren't always the best behaved, and my husband kind of forgot about me sometimes, and then, of course, there was my boss—she was a piece of work. But misery? Seems a little dramatic now, doesn't it?"

Her companion laughed. Not just a chuckle, but a throw-back-your-head, mile-wide, Julia Roberts kind of laugh. "I know! I know! Weren't we such babies? I mean, yes, I did get in that car accident when I was fifteen, and I was never the same, it's true. And there was that incident with that guy in college who stalked me. And then of course a thousand other terrible things. And they were terrible. Sometimes they seemed like more than any one person could bear, you know? But I survived. And now. . .I mean, look at us now!"

Both women laughed then, out of pure joy. Then the first woman turned a bit more thoughtful. "Do you think—I mean—if anyone had tried to tell us then, would we have listened? Would you have listened? I remember long ago my mother trying to tell me something when I was a teenager. I had just been dumped by this guy I thought was *the* guy—he seemed like my whole world for about seven months of my life—and I was sobbing in my room. She came in and sat on my bed and put her hand on my back. I remember her hand there, how it stilled something inside me. And she said, 'I know it doesn't seem like it now, but this will pass. It really isn't the end of your world.' But I didn't believe her. I mean, I fiercely and actively did not believe her."

"But she was right. You could see that even then, couldn't you?" her friend asked. She nodded in reply. "I think that's what we do sometimes, down there. We hold on to our stories so tightly. We want to think we're in control and we've got it all figured out—for good or bad. But He's the One in charge. He's holding us. And He's writing stories for us that are so much better than we could ever imagine."

"So much better. They aren't even comparable!" And the two friends laughed again as they walked into the heavenly light.

♥ · ♥ · ♥ · ·

*Lord, help me to glimpse Your glory and keep
walking in the story You are writing for me. Amen.*

Like a Tree

"But blessed is the one who trusts in the LORD,
whose confidence is in him."
JEREMIAH 17:7

The pear trees grew golden as the air changed. Their fruit swung heavy on the branches, filled with sweet goodness. When the winds blew in the late-summer storm, the leaves held on for dear life—determined to finish their fuel-producing cycle before they gave up and began to fall. The trees stood tall and strong, with branches curving gracefully to the sky. Their roots grabbed tightly to the ground, spreading out and reaching for the nearby stream for refreshment. Year after year, the trees had grown and provided fruit for anyone who visited the farm. And year after year, their beauty blessed everyone who saw them.

But a few fields away, a once-beautiful pear tree stood on an abandoned estate. It had been planted in a container so it could be placed in a particular spot according to the grand design of the owner. Its growth had been stunted as a result. Then, when the owner's fortunes turned and he was no longer able to maintain the large gardens, he packed up the few belongings he could still call his own and went on his way, leaving all his beautiful plants to fend for themselves. It took only a few months for most of the estate to become an overgrown wilderness, and the poor trees and other plants in containers, without access to water (as the season was a dry one), began to shrivel and bend themselves in grotesque curves.

So it goes with our hearts. As the Lord told the prophet Jeremiah, those who put their trust mainly in mankind—whose hearts turn away from the Lord and who depend on people for fulfillment and happiness—will not be strong, but instead will suffer like bushes in a barren wasteland. Empty promises will disappoint such people, and they won't find solid ground in which to plant their hopes. There will be no steady source of food and refreshment for them, and thus they will be unable to bear fruit—to produce the kind of growth and behaviors that are needed to do good for others and for themselves.

But those who put their roots deep into the foundation of faith, hope, and love that the Lord provides us will have endurance and perseverance. Even when drought comes and hard times make it difficult to push through, their relationship with the Lord will help them be strong and confident. And they will never fail to bear good fruit.

Lord, thank You for being a never-ending source
of refreshment and strength for me. Amen.

Better Together

For none of us lives for ourselves alone, and none of us dies for ourselves alone.

ROMANS 14:7

. . . .

Kathy was positively driven to succeed. She made sure her record in school and at her job was spotless, so that when she applied to graduate school the only question would be how much, not whether, scholarship money would be offered.

In contrast, Kathy didn't see much use in investing in people, unless they had something to offer her. Friends and boyfriends and all of that could wait for later, she felt.

The one person Kathy spent time with was her mother, Beth. Kathy's parents were divorced long ago, and her mother supported her on her own. Beth had worked hard to send Kathy to the best schools she could afford. She loved her daughter very much. Kathy loved her mother too, but she didn't understand her. She wanted a better life for herself than what her mother had—much better.

One Sunday, Kathy bumped into a close friend of her mother's. Jill was a successful lawyer, and Kathy was glad to see her. They decided to go for coffee.

As Jill watched Kathy order, she remembered a recent chat she'd had with Beth, and how worried she was about Kathy—about her obsession with school and work. As they sat down, Jill listened to Kathy list off her recent accomplishments and all the places she intended to apply to.

Jill asked, "What's it all for, though?"

Kathy cocked her head. "What do you mean? It's so I can be successful at life—have a life that's worth something, that's better than—"

"—better than your mother's?" Jill asked. Kathy just stirred the foam on top of her coffee, disturbing the barista's artwork. Jill put her hand out to Kathy. "Look, Kathy. I love you like my own, but I'm going to tell you something. If you really want to be a success, look at your mother. She is smart and capable— she could have done any number of things with her life. She gave up a lot for you. She goes to church and prays for you. Why? Because you are what makes her life meaningful. You are what makes her life worth something. Not because of your grades or some job you might land one day, but just because you are you—you are her daughter. And you are valuable."

A tear dropped from Kathy's eye, making a perfect little brown circle appear in the white foam in her cup.

Jill went on, "None of us is put here just for ourselves. No one is born that way, and no one dies that way. We are here to be together. And that's what makes our lives better."

Lord, help me live for others. Amen.

Not Sacrifice

For I desire faithful love and not sacrifice,
the knowledge of God rather than burnt offerings.
HOSEA 6:6 CSB

. . . .

Charlie was a good father, as far as he understood himself. He had come from a tough background, in which he was raised by his single father. His father had done what he could for him, but "what he could" was limited by his father's own needs and indulgences. As a boy and an adolescent, Charlie had seen more than either a boy or an adolescent ought to see.

In the course of time, Charlie managed to meet a lovely girl, Patty, and they married and had a family of three children, two girls and a boy. Over the years, he was determined to give his family more stability than he'd had when he was a boy. He was especially determined to shield his son from some of the things that he had seen when he was growing up. Some of that was accomplished by the fact that he had a stable marriage, but Charlie took much of it on his shoulders. He was going to play by the rules that everybody else played by and give his children a solid upbringing. He sent them to Christian schools and took them to church every Sunday. He worked hard to give them everything they needed and many of the things they wanted.

But one day, Charlie came upon his eldest child, Lila, sitting quietly. He asked her what she was thinking about. At first, she just gave him a perfunctory, "Nothing." But Charlie could see that something was on her mind, something was bothering her.

"Come on, Lila. What's going on?" After a minute or so, she started gushing. "At school today, the teacher was talking about how God loves us, and how God loves everybody. I don't believe that. Nobody loves me." Lila hid her face in her hands.

Charlie put his arm around her. "That's not true," he said. "I love you."

"No, you don't," Lila countered. "All you ever do is work and watch television and stuff. You never do anything with us." And she sobbed harder. Charlie sat stunned. He looked around at all the material resources he had provided. He'd thought all of that would tell his family how much he loved them. But as Lila leaned into his chest, Charlie knew his sacrifices were not sufficient. Lila didn't want his sacrifices; she wanted his love. Charlie held her tighter, whispering, "I'm so sorry, Lila. I'm so sorry. I love you. I always will love you."

Father God, I love You. I want to show
You that every day. Help me know how. Amen.

What Do I Owe?

*Don't run up debts, except for the huge
debt of love you owe each other.*
ROMANS 13:8 MSG

. . . .

"What do I owe you?" The question arises often in matters of simple exchange, a purchase of some sort or other. That kind of owing, that temporary and quickly eliminated kind, is only one kind of the owing we experience. Materially, we can owe on a large scale—mortgages and tuition and the like. And then there are the immaterial debts. We owe respect to our superiors and bosses and parents; to these latter we also owe honor and love. During the holidays, when we might be exhausted and not feeling much like bringing the children to visit their grandparents, we do so because we think we owe it to the grandparents.

Paul makes us ask ourselves another question though: Am I surrendering and giving up to others the love that I owe—the one debt, so to speak, that I really ought to be paying off? Let's listen to the story of Carrie.

Carrie had a family of three small children of school age, nine, seven, and five—all boys. She and her husband lived several hundred miles from her mother, who lived in the same town as Carrie's brother. Her mother lived alone in the small house in which she had raised her family, and she was failing mentally. Carrie's brother, Pete, tried to visit her as much as he could, but he was busy with work, and he didn't get along well with their mother. To him, taking care of her was almost strictly a debt.

At Christmastime, Carrie made a concerted effort to get the boys little elf outfits to wear to visit their grandma. Her mother had a real fondness for the holiday and had often dolled up her own children in a similar fashion when they were very small. Carrie was pretty excited when she and the children and the presents were stuffed into their van for the trip. Her enthusiasm was contagious, so the children were excited too, and her husband, Jeff, smiled broadly at her, shaking his head at her joy. Off they all went on their four-hour drive to her mother's house. When they arrived, the children spilled out of the vehicle to ring the bell and greet their elderly grandmother.

Carrie was thrilled when she witnessed the look of surprise and pleasure on the face of her mother, who exclaimed, "Well, look at my beautiful little elves!"

Carrie experienced the joy that comes with giving toward the one debt that we all truly owe—loving another one of God's children.

*God, I want to be generous in paying off my debt of
love to others. Help me to give easily and often. Amen.*

Chosen

*"You did not choose me, but I chose you and appointed
you so that you might go and bear fruit—fruit that will last—
and so that whatever you ask in my name the Father will give you."*
JOHN 15:16

In the course of salvation history, we find many figures whose lives were claimed by God for His purposes. Mary the mother of Jesus comes to mind, along with Joseph her husband, Elizabeth her cousin, John the Baptist, and the list goes on. Somehow, the question of "What are you going to do with your life?" does not appear to have been a question for those human beings. God chose them, and He chose them for a specific reason and purpose, in such a manner that everything else in their lives pales in comparison.

Mel was reflecting on this line that Jesus had spoken to His disciples at the Last Supper: "You did not choose me, but I chose you." Mel was seventy-five years old now, and he had a son, Jackie, who was fifty and suffered from polio. Jackie had been confined to a wheelchair all his life, and his muscles were gradually weakening as he aged. That meant he needed more and more help as time went on. Jackie's parents were themselves getting on in years, and it grew increasingly harder for them to meet his needs. Fortunately, they had two other children, Sarah and Naomi, who were very generous, and whose own children were happy to help out when they were needed.

Mel thought about his own life. God had given him a beautiful son, disabled as he was. Jackie was generally a cheerful person, and he didn't take the help of the people around him for granted. He had worked when he could. Sometimes the two of them would sit and read the Bible or pray together. God had also given Mel and his wife two caring and loving daughters. What was it that God had called them to do, he mused, except to be loving and caring toward this one common center of their lives? Was there anything else that any of them had done that in the end was storing up treasure in heaven? Sure, the girls had their children, but they were off living their own lives for the most part. Had they learned this thing that he had come to learn? Did they understand the special privilege, the beauty, of what God had given them in their uncle? The beauty of helping another human being thrive? Mel dozed off in his chair reflecting peacefully on how God had chosen him and hoping fervently that he had borne fruit that would last.

Lord, help me to recognize what You have chosen me to do. Amen.

Always Prepared

But in your hearts revere Christ as Lord. Always be prepared to give an answer to everyone who asks you to give the reason for the hope that you have.
1 PETER 3:15

Hal had spent much of his life keeping to himself. "Mind your own business" was his motto for daily living. He was a good man, a caring father, and a loving husband, but he mostly just kept his head down and tried not to get too involved in people's lives. He loved and followed Jesus, but he didn't talk about that much either—he didn't think people would really want to hear about it.

That all changed when cancer struck.

A friend asked Hal about this one day. "Hal, I've been noticing something about you. You've become more outspoken, and lately, you speak out for a purpose—and that purpose just seems to be friendly to people, to encourage them. But it's more than that, I guess. I mean, you seem to be spending a lot of time telling people about Jesus and urging them to get to know Him. Why are you so, so. . ."

"Evangelistic?" Hal finished for his friend. "That's easy. I figure I don't have much time left. And the most important thing I could possibly do with the time that I have is share the hope that I have with others. That hope is the best part of me. It's that hope that lets me love my family. It's that hope that helps me love others and want good things for them. And from my point of view now—as someone who is trying to come to grips with the idea that I'm leaving this world soon and going to live with God—really the only thing that is worth doing at all is sharing the hope that I have. So I might as well share it with as many people as I can."

And that's exactly what he did. Hal shared the good news of Jesus with the nurses in the chemo clinic. He shared it with every doctor he met. He shared it with the radiologist. He went out and knocked on doors of neighbors he had been only nodding at on the street for twenty years, and he shared it with them and made new friends in the last days of his life. Up until the very end, when his disease finally took away his voice and his breath, Hal spent every waking moment making sure every person he encountered knew how much he loved them, and how much God did too.

*Lord, help me not to wait too long
to share the hope that I have. Amen.*

Light of the World

"I am the light of the world. Whoever follows me will never walk in darkness, but will have the light of life."
JOHN 8:12

On foggy mornings, the sun rises as usual—just like any other day. But instead of the world waking up and acknowledging its arrival, the low, thick clouds blot out its light. But the light is still there. The world is not dark. Light scatters through the particles of the clouds, blanketing the world in gray. As the sun rises and the temperature of the air grows warmer, the clouds begin to move, rising away from the earth. Soon, shafts of light come breaking through the clouds, dazzling us with a golden glow.

The light of our world is sometimes hard for us to see, but it is always there, and it never leaves us in darkness.

Jesus claimed to be the light of the world. The Pharisees He spoke to were blinded by the clouds of their own pride and knowledge—they wanted to be right. They wanted to be in control. So they tried to challenge Jesus' authority. But they ultimately failed, because the light of Jesus' truth shone through their questioning.

It was Jesus' light that shone down on the woman caught in adultery—putting her in the spotlight, not to shame her, but to feature her as a symbol of the hypocrisy of those standing ready to accuse her (John 8:1–11). He shone on her to give her grace. He shone on her to warm her in His light and let her know He would not condemn her.

It was Jesus' light that drew people to Him in the temple courts, where He taught about who He was and about the Father who had sent Him. He taught that He would soon have to leave this world, but those who would follow Him, who would keep seeking the light of life, would not be left to die in the darkness of their sins.

It is Jesus' light that shines in our lives still today. It is His light that draws us to Him. It is His light that we stand in to confess our sins and be forgiven. It is His light that sets us free. We may not see it clearly. At times we may even get caught up in our own confusion and pride and impatiently claim we do not see it. But in those times, we have to hold on to the knowledge that His light is always there, ready to break through our clouds.

Lord, be the light in my darkest moments. Amen.

You must each decide in your heart how much to give. And don't give reluctantly or in response to pressure. "For God loves a person who gives cheerfully."
2 Corinthians 9:7 nlt

Jimmy was in the church hall working on the combination food giveaway and soup kitchen. For several hours he had pitched in wherever he could. He bagged the food donations for a while, then worked with the lines of needy people. He worked in the dining area, clearing off tables and getting the patrons the various things they needed. He worked for a while in the kitchen, cleaning utensils and collecting trash.

Jimmy had come into the hall in the morning determined to help out as much as he possibly could. He was a soldier for Jesus, and he planned to exhaust himself by the end of the drive. But as the day wore on, fatigue set in and his determination waned, along with his spirits. At one point he took a break from his efforts and asked Jesus to give him strength to finish the day.

While on break, he noticed another person serving. Betty was a woman around Jimmy's age, thirtysomething, and she had spent a good deal of the early hours dishing out food to the patrons, a job that was difficult due to the need to keep on a cheerful face even as your legs grew weary from standing and yours arms cramped up from serving the food. Moreover, the job required a lot of concentration. But Betty was equal to the task. She smiled her way through a couple of hours at the food counter. She helped to bag groceries for a while too, before turning to the task of dealing with the needy public again.

Every time Jimmy saw her, she wore a natural, happy smile. Later, Jimmy stopped Betty to ask about her day. He remarked, "You sure looked happy to be here today."

She chuckled a little. "If you want to know the truth," she replied, "I've been very happy to be here. And I can tell you why."

"That, I would like to hear," Jimmy retorted as they left the hall.

"I'm happy because Jesus identifies with these people. That's what He says; He identifies with the least of His brothers. So I keep thinking that I'm serving Jesus every time I interact with one of the patrons. And that's why I think God loves a cheerful giver. God loves the giver who smiles when she is giving to His Son."

And now Jimmy was smiling too.

God, I want to give all that I can for You. Help me to leave behind my own worries and needs and to give of the best of me. Amen.

Quick, Slow, Slow

*Understand this, my dear brothers and sisters: You must
all be quick to listen, slow to speak, and slow to get angry.
Human anger does not produce the righteousness God desires.*
JAMES 1:19–20 NLT

You get in the car and start the morning commute. Wham! You slam on the brakes as some person with an apparent death wish decides to cut in front of you in their extremely big hurry to. . .wait for it. . .the very next exit. After your heart stops pounding, you continue on, but miss the turn you've taken every day for the last ten years because you just realized that you also slammed your coffee cup out of the holder and onto the floor, just out of reach of your fingertips.

And all the while you've been muttering various choice words, the little ears in the backseat have been listening to every single syllable. You look at your young son in the rearview mirror and say, "Sorry, Jacob! Mommy's having a hard morning."

"So it's okay to say things like that when it's a bad day?" Jacob can always be counted on to put things in perspective.

"No, it's not okay, buddy. I'm sorry. I just let my words come out too fast. I'll try harder."

"That's okay, Mommy. Daddy does it too."

Quick to listen. Slow to speak. Slow to get angry. It sounds pretty easy, doesn't it? But to whom should we listen? And what should we be speaking? What will produce righteousness, after all?

We should be quick to listen to God and to His Word, which we should have planted in our hearts. Especially in heated moments when we are prone to anger, we should listen to God reminding us to be patient, to think things through, to consider others above ourselves.

Be slow to speak. Slow to speak the first thing that comes to your mind. Those first things hardly ever represent the truth of who you are, or even the truth of what you really think.

Be slow to get angry. God's anger comes from the place where all good things come from. God loves us with a pure form of love that always has our best interests at heart. His anger is incurred when His children are treated unjustly, or when they disobey Him and hurt one another. But humans get angry for all sorts of reasons that have very little to do with love. Yet if we follow God's example, we can find the way to righteousness. And keep ourselves from being a bad example to the kids in the backseat.

Lord, slow my tongue. And quicken my heart to be aligned with Yours. Amen.

Desire and Power

For God is working in you, giving you the desire and the power to do what pleases him.
Do everything without complaining and arguing, so that no one can criticize you.
Live clean, innocent lives as children of God.
PHILIPPIANS 2:13–15 NLT

We can't do this without God. That's all there is to it.

What is "this"? "This" is everything—anything that's worthwhile, anything that can make a difference in the world. "This" is how we are meant to shine brightly for Christ.

No complaining? No arguing? No one criticizing you? In most households with teenagers, this by itself would be some kind of miracle. Can you imagine being able to go about your daily routine, making plans for where you need to go, what you need to buy, and what you are making for dinner, without someone trying to negate your votes? Can you imagine making it through a day in which you yourself don't complain about something?

Living a clean, innocent life? So we shine like a bright light "in a world full of crooked and perverse people" (Philippians 2:15 NLT)? Does that sound anything at all like something you could achieve on your own? Does that even sound like something you'd choose to do on a normal day?

How about rejoicing even if we lose everything? Does that sound like an achievable goal for most of us? How do we even begin to learn how to do that? How do we make our service an acceptable offering to God? Should we make a practice of losing things just so we can experiment with personal failure?

Can you hold firmly to the Word of life? Can you obey the Creator's words—the words of the One who made all things well and designed them to function together in a beautiful harmony? Can you listen to where He leads you so that your work will not be useless? Can you follow in His steps, looking out for ways to solve problems creatively and to work together with others in wisdom and grace?

We *can* do all of "this." We can do these things because the One who made us *is* working within us and through us, not just to make us capable and competent, but to make us *want* to do what pleases Him. And when we have the desire to please Him, and the power to please Him, we will be able to meet the goal of pleasing Him. And then we will certainly rejoice.

Creator God, thank You for the wonderful
working You perform in me! Amen.

Least

*"Truly I tell you, whatever you did for one of the least
of these brothers and sisters of mine, you did for me."*
Matthew 25:40

Living in a world of front-runners, of superstars and celebrities and anchors and authors, the people at the other end of the spectrum seem almost antlike. Indeed, in the face of all the bright lights and the microphones, one can hardly be blamed for the temptation to ask, "Do those little people matter at all?"

Andy thought about that a lot as he drove through the city to work and back home. He could hardly help thinking about it. At every stoplight it seemed there were people, male and female, young and old, with a sign, with a hand out, with a look that would wrench the heart out of even a zombie, and they ruined him. They broke his heart every day without fail. And so he began a personal crusade. He armed himself with answers to their prayers. He made sure he left home and office with cash, not a fortune, just twenty dollars or so in ones and fives. And he gave alms. He rolled down his window at stoplights and gave them the help they asked of him. It didn't always make him *feel* better, but it always felt better than doing nothing or ignoring the people begging.

Sometimes when he was in his car with a friend or colleague, they would ask him about what he was doing or challenge him. "Why are you throwing your money away? They're just going to get a drink or a fix." Andy never knew how to respond to those admonitions. He only knew that there in front of him was a human being, made in the image and likeness of God, according to what he believed, and that human being was begging him. Sometimes he would ask his critic, "What am I supposed to do, come equipped with a form for them to fill out? Ask them how often they get donations and what they do with them?" For him, it was a simple affair: either you give, or you don't.

One story that drove Andy forward in his crusade was the story of Jesus separating the sheep from the goats. What did Jesus have to say to His listeners? "Whatever you did for one of the least of these brothers and sisters of mine, you did for me." Jesus did not identify with His friends in the passenger seat with their tidy advice. Jesus identified with the people on the median strip, the least of these. Jesus loved from the ground up.

Jesus, help me to love as freely and easily as You do. Amen.

Offer Up

*Use your whole body as an instrument to
do what is right for the glory of God.*
ROMANS 6:13 NLT

· ·

Caroline stretched out her arm and traced the blue lines of her veins from her shoulder down to her wrist. Her skin had always been so pale. She remembered once, a long time ago, tracing her own mother's veins in the same way, and asking her why she had made blue marker lines on her skin. Her mother had laughed.

That was long before the bruises started appearing on the inside of her mother's wrist, in the size and shape of tightly gripping fingers. Long before the constant yelling. Long before her father finally left the house and didn't come back. And long before Caroline started self-medicating with whatever alcohol she could find.

But today felt different. Today Caroline felt like she was standing on the edge of some invisible cliff, ready to leap off into a new part of her life. She wanted to be "dead to sin" and "alive to God," as she had heard the speaker say in the group meeting the other night. She wanted that as badly as she had ever wanted another buzz. She wanted to put behind her a past that was filled with decisions made based solely on temporary, selfish wants. And she wanted not to want things that would only hurt her, or hurt other people. But could she achieve this? Not on her own, that was for certain.

So why am I here now? Caroline wondered, as the stranger stretched the rubbery strip around her arm and pressed softly on her flesh, feeling for the vein. *Why do this now?*

The needle went in quickly with just a slight sting. Caroline relaxed and laid her head back. She smiled. She knew why. Because it felt good to be doing something good with her body. It felt good to offer herself up to a path that led toward life. To offer someone else a bit of life-giving force.

"Thanks so much for your donation, Caroline," the nurse said, handing Caroline some informational sheets. "Take it easy today, okay?"

Yes, easy, thought Caroline. *It's not been an easy road to get here, but it's easy to want to offer every part of me up to God.* She walked out under the huge BLOOD DRIVE TODAY sign, eating the last bites of her complimentary cookie and smiling from ear to ear.

♥ · · ❤ · · ▶ · · ·

*Lord God, thank You for allowing me to start with a new slate.
Help me know how to use every part of me to glorify You. Amen.*

Encouraging Hope

Then we will be with the Lord forever.
So encourage each other with these words.
1 Thessalonians 4:17–18 nlt

Sometimes living on this planet is just hard to bear. We look around and become weighed down by the gravity of the grave. People are shot and killed every day, for reasons of vengefulness and hatred and wickedness—and sometimes for no reason at all. People do horrible things to each other in the name of desire or some twisted version of what they call love. And they don't even know it's twisted, because it's impossible for them to see a straight path—much less walk one. People do terrible, sickening things to weak, helpless individuals—and one wonders if evil is winning after all. Perhaps the demons have got the upper hand.

But that's not how it is. Not at all. And we must not let ourselves be so absorbed in seeing evil that we forget to look for the light. The light is always there. The light is always shining. The light is, in fact, the reason we feel so appalled at the darkness.

So when we grieve, we can know that, yes, it is okay to be sad. When people we love leave this world, it is perfectly acceptable to miss them. But we should not despair—as if the leaving of one good man or woman somehow subtracts that amount of goodness from our environment. We have not lost their goodness. We have not really even lost them—they are simply away from us for a while.

As Christians, we can be sure that those who have accepted Jesus as their Savior will truly be saved. They will be saved from the darkness of this world, but they will also be saved from the darkness of death. They will not disappear. We all can have this hope. Whether we have already passed before Jesus comes again, or whether we are still standing on this ground when He returns. We will all be caught up together with Jesus. We all will rise. We all will be freed from suffering and selfishness and the sin of this dark world. We will start new stories with Jesus. We will learn new songs. We will see what happens when goodness rules in every corner of the universe.

It is this hope that we live in. It is this hope we can take with us as we live and work and breathe in this world. It is this hope we can be secure in, even when we are sitting in a funeral service. Darkness has not won. Look for the light.

Lord, I want to encourage others with the hope that I have.
Help me find the words to do that. Amen.

Never Separated

For I am convinced that neither death nor life, neither angels nor demons, neither the present nor the future, nor any powers, neither height nor depth, nor anything else in all creation, will be able to separate us from the love of God that is in Christ Jesus our Lord.
<small>ROMANS 8:38–39</small>

Imagine for a minute that you live in a world of fear. Imagine that every bump in the night, every problem in your path, every bad thing that happens—no matter how big or small—seems to be one more bit of evidence of not just bad things happening to you, but bad spirits out to get you. Imagine that every day you struggle just to step outside your door because you are so afraid of what might happen.

Anxiety can be a powerful force. It can tie people up just as surely as if heavy chains were locked around them. It can make people feel as if they are physically heavy. It can trap people in their homes as if boulders have been moved in front of their doors. It can imprison people inside their own minds.

But God is stronger. And God can set people free.

Many people are trapped within themselves due to anxiety, and they don't even know it. It's important for this reason for all of us to keep reaching out to each other. It's important for us to care for one another and be in each other's lives enough to be able to ask, "Are you okay?" And it's important for us to be able to know when the answer to that question is truthful or not.

It can be messy to be in each other's lives. It can be extremely difficult to help someone suffering with a mental illness. But it is also one of the most beautiful things to see someone who was once a slave to fear be freed and able to live again. Wise treatment plans will include not only medicines but also the assurance of support—the acknowledgment that other people need to stay in the patient's life.

Because the truth is, we all need to be reminded that we are not alone. That we are never ever alone. That nothing can separate us from the love of good people, and nothing can keep us away from the love of Christ. No troubles. No bumps in the night. No bad people. No illness. No persecution. No physical conditions. No mental conditions. No demons. No distance. Absolutely nothing can keep us from God's eternal, powerful, pure, forgiving love.

*Lord, help me reach out to others and
remind them that they are never far from You. Amen.*

Against God

*"How then could I do such a wicked
thing and sin against God?"*
GENESIS 39:9

The one factor in Joseph's life that made all the difference in the way he lived—that allowed him to move up the ranks of Egyptian society, from slave to second-in-command—was his recognition of the fact that God was with him.

God was with him in the bottom of the pit where his brothers had thrown him. God was with him when he was sold as a slave. God was with him when he was placed in Potiphar's house. God was with him in prison. God was with him when he was called to stand before Pharaoh. God was with him in his visions. God was with him in his decisions. God was always with Joseph.

But if Joseph had not known this, and been grateful for it, his life might have turned out very differently.

When Joseph was bought by Potiphar, he probably didn't even realize how powerful his master was at first. Potiphar was an official in the Egyptian ruling class—he was captain of the guard. He was used to people following his orders. And he was good at spotting leaders. Potiphar saw a leader in Joseph. He trusted Joseph. Potiphar could see that Joseph was favored by God. And Joseph knew that God was blessing him in everything he did. The more he realized God's favor, no doubt the more Joseph wanted to serve the Lord and honor and obey Him.

So when Joseph found himself in a tricky situation with his master's wife, Joseph knew what he had to do. He refused to be with the woman, even though she commanded him to sleep with her.

Joseph knew that if he did this thing, it would not just be a breach of trust with his master. It would not just be a bad thing to do to the man who had trusted him with everything he owned. It would in fact be a sin against God.

Sometimes we find ourselves in sticky situations. It can be very difficult to decide what to do. Sometimes it might even seem as though we can't escape temptation. But one thing that can help us get out of this kind of trouble is the knowledge and certainty of the fact that God is with us. God is the reason we are where we are. God is the reason that any good thing has happened to us at all. If we give in to temptation and commit acts of sin, we are not just doing bad things to others or ourselves; we are sinning against God.

Lord, help me. I don't ever want to sin against You. Amen.

Walking Partners

Do two walk together unless they have agreed to do so?
Amos 3:3

Louise seemed to wear a permanent frown. Deep lines were etched into the folds around her mouth, giving her the appearance of something like a wooden puppet. One wondered, though, whether even a master ventriloquist could make her say any good thing at all. It seemed like her lips wouldn't allow a pleasant word to escape.

"Misery loves company," people would mutter when speaking of Louise. And misery did seem to be Louise's constant companion. She was known as the town complainer. Whenever any new program was proposed, Louise would send in a letter to the editor of the local paper, describing why the plan was, in her words, "idiotic," "a waste of everyone's time and tax money," and "a fool's errand."

Louise was the kind of woman who didn't need a watch-dog, because she herself barked at every small child, delivery person, or stray twig that dared to land in her lawn. Over the years, Louise's family had gradually either moved away or passed away, and of course, she had no friends, so she kept to herself much of the time.

When Jenny moved in next door to Louise, she was happy to see the tidy little lawn with the pretty pansies planted in neat beds. She figured Louise would be a good neighbor since she clearly cared so well for her home. Jenny popped over to Louise's front door with some homemade muffins, hoping to make a friend.

Louise cracked open her door in answer to Jenny's knock. "Who are you? What do you want?"

Jenny didn't let the gruff questions bother her. "Hi. I've just moved in. We're going to be neighbors! And I wanted to offer you some muffins as my way of saying hello."

Louise's arthritic paw poked out through the crack and grabbed the plate of muffins. "Fine. But don't come back here. I don't need any new friends." And just like that, the muffins and Louise disappeared.

Jenny decided then and there that what Louise needed was a new walking partner. *That woman has cuddled up with loneliness too long*, Jenny thought. She knew what that was like. She had spent a long time shut away from the world after her husband passed away. Jenny asked God to help her get through to Louise. And after that, Jenny knocked on Louise's door every day until the woman finally let her in.

Now the two of them can be seen strolling through town most days. And sometimes, Louise is even smiling.

*Lord, help me not to become so familiar with my troubles that
I shut out the world of people You have for me to love. Amen.*

Harmony

*Rejoice with those who rejoice; mourn with those
who mourn. Live in harmony with one another.*
Romans 12:15–16

The choir director was getting frustrated. Everyone could tell. "Try it again," she sighed, sounding more than a little defeated.

The singers obeyed. Some voices were reaching for notes and not finding them—not even in the same universe, it seemed. Some voices were straining to cover up colds. Some were just too tentative. Some were loud and strong, but completely in the wrong spot.

Nancy, a relatively new recruit, piped up after the few measures had thankfully been cut off by the weary director. "Ms. Rosalind, I read something about this song that I thought was interesting."

"Yes? Go ahead—everyone, relax for a minute."

"Well, I read that the composer wrote this song after his infant girl had died." There were some sympathetic moans at this news, and some whispers of "Why on earth is she telling us this?" But Nancy continued. "He said he wanted to write something to capture the feeling he had as he was holding her in his arms as she faded away. He matched his breath to hers on purpose. In. . .out. In. . .out. Because he wanted to feel that even after she was gone, he could be with her—he could remember her with every breath. He could remember the life she gave him and his wife, no matter how short it was, and could breathe that life into his work and his care of his family, and his art. He said that this song is all about the breathing. The breathing supports the harmony—the song is born out of that union. He wrote the chords before anything else for that reason. It's all about the harmony."

The room had become quite still as Nancy was speaking. The singers were seated on the platform and some now had tears in their eyes.

Ms. Rosalind rose quietly, motioning everyone to stay seated. She held up her hand and directed the choir to sing the first chord of the first measure with no words—just one unified, open "Ah." She directed them through the next chord and the next, until they had moved through every chord of the song. And as they sang, each voice got stronger. The harmonies became tighter. The chord changes became sharper.

The director had them hold out the final note for a long time, then motioned for them to stop. She looked at Nancy. "Thank you, dear. Thank you for reminding us. It's all about the harmony."

Lord, help me to harmonize my life with the lives of others so I can show compassion. Amen.

Not about You

*"But when you give to the needy, do not let your left hand know
what your right hand is doing, so that your giving may be in secret.
Then your Father, who sees what is done in secret, will reward you."*
MATTHEW 6:3–4

In Matthew 6, Jesus teaches about several behaviors of those who would seek to follow Him. This whole part of the Sermon on the Mount easily could have been labeled "It's Not about You."

He tells us to give in secret—not to be seen. Why? Because it's not about you. It's not about how much you have to give or how generous you are. It's not about your righteousness. It's about honoring God by taking care of His people.

Jesus tells us to pray in secret—not out on the street corners to be heard by every passerby. Why not? Isn't it a good thing to pray in public? Sure—but this is not about you. Your daily prayer life should be about the time you spend in intimate relationship with God. It's not about making a speech. It's not about showing others how well you can pray or how holy you are. There's no word count quota. God knows what you need and want. He just wants to spend time with you.

Similarly, fasting should not be done as a show of suffering. Only God needs to know about what you are giving, and for how long, and why. When you commit to depending on Him, really commit to depending on Him—not on your own image.

Jesus goes on to warn us about where we store our treasures—are we serving our stuff or are we serving our Savior? Are we piling up things to show our success? Or are we concerned instead about being successful citizens of heaven?

Lastly, worry does not appear at first as a form of pride, but it is. When you worry about the things of this life, you take your eyes off God. You worry because on some level you think you can figure out all the answers—you can supply your own needs. But God wants you to depend on Him. He wants you to lean on Him. It's just not about you. And it's not about just you. It's about where you are with God.

*Lord, help me to remember that whatever I do to follow You,
I should be following You and not trying to lead my own way.
Help me to depend on You above all else. Amen.*

Schedules

*Instead, you ought to say, "If it is the Lord's will,
we will live and do this or that."*
JAMES 4:15

6:00 a.m. Wake up. Start coffee. Start breakfast. Pack lunches. 6:30 a.m. Wake up first child. 7:00 a.m. Wake up second child. 7:30 a.m. Take first child to school. 8:00 a.m. Take second child to school. 8:30 a.m. Go to work. 9:00–10:30 a.m. Meetings. 11:30 a.m. Stop for lunch. Work through lunch. 12:30–3:00 p.m. More meetings. 3:00–5:30 p.m. More work and pick up children from sitter. 6:00 p.m. Go home. Start dinner. 7:00 p.m. Eat dinner. 7:30 p.m. Check homework. Help with homework. 8:30 p.m. Help children get ready for bed. 10:00 p.m. Go to bed.

6:00 a.m. Start again.

Where in our schedules is a designated time for God? Do we compare our calendars with His? Do we talk with Him about where He wants us to go? Or do we ignore what He has to say to us about our daily practices?

Is the time we set aside to spend with God during the week enough? How do we know? How do we find out? And if it's not enough, what are we going to do about it?

Sometimes our trouble begins right at the beginning. It begins when we don't even remember to make room for God. It begins when we forget to thank Him for any time that we have. It begins when we forget that all of our moments, all of our ins and outs and backs and forths and tos and fros—all of it belongs to Him.

What if, instead of to-do lists, we created to-don'ts? What if we started each day by remembering all the things we would not do, could not do, except that God wills it to be so? What if we started our schedules with a thank-you note to our Father, instead of ending each day with a hurried good night to God? What if we remembered that we should make every step count for Him, because Jesus made every step on earth count for us—including each step on the way to the cross.

There's nothing wrong with making plans and being organized. But there's everything wrong with not including God in our plans. There's everything wrong with forgetting the work He has for us to do first—the work of loving Him and loving one another. That has to come first. Everything else can be rescheduled.

*Lord, don't let me get so carried away with my calendar that I forget that
every day is a day You made, and I should be glad and grateful for it. Amen.*

Knock

"Ask and it will be given to you; seek and you will find;
knock and the door will be opened to you."
MATTHEW 7:7

Al had never been much of a churchgoing man. If you asked him, he'd tell you he never got much out of it. But then there came a season when his family went through a crisis, and Al wished he understood more about God. Al and his wife, Bess, had two sons, one almost graduated from college and the other with a couple of years to go. When Trey, the elder son, was in his final semester of college, Al and Bess discovered that he had been using drugs and, indeed, had something of a habit. At first they were completely frantic about the news. But after a short time, they decided to get their son whatever help they could.

First, they sent him to a therapist in the hope that counseling might bring him around. Of course, at home they watched him like a hawk. They were both anxious all the time—never knowing for certain whether he was hiding things from them or not. But they couldn't watch him all the time. After a while, it became clear that Trey still wasn't completely clean. So they sent him to an outpatient program and continued to watch and wait. At home he was fairly lethargic. He slept a lot.

Al pressed him to look for work, but it was like pulling teeth trying to get him out of bed in the morning. He and Bess were increasingly alarmed about what would become of him, but they waited.

One Friday morning when Al went to wake him, he stood over him, watching his boy sleep, remembering the little face he had watched when Trey was just a newborn. And as he watched, he felt suddenly a wave of sadness mixed with fear. The worried father whispered softly, "Oh God, I don't know what to do. I don't know what to do. Please help me." And he went and sat in a nearby chair, tears in his eyes. He felt the fear and sadness replaced by a warm sensation, something like peace. He went to church the following Sunday—he felt he owed it to God. And he continued to attend ever after that Sunday.

He told Bess about it later, saying he felt like he had spoken to God and God had spoken back to him that Friday morning. Like he had been waiting and waiting for something to happen to Trey and instead, something happened to him. He felt like he had knocked, and the door opened.

Lord, I am asking, I am seeking, I am knocking.
Please open the door wide and let me see You. Amen.

Love Covers

Above all, love each other deeply,
because love covers over a multitude of sins.
1 PETER 4:8

Dirty socks on the living room floor. The used-up toilet roll left on the dispenser. . .again. Crumbs in the bed. Toothpaste globs on the bathroom sink.

Can love cover over all of that? Yes.

Now, to be fair, none of those things in the list above are really sins. But these day-to-day annoyances we deal with when we live with other humans are often the things that lead to sins—sins such as self-centeredness, deceit ("No, I didn't eat the last piece of cake!"), envy, and even hatred. One trivial mistake can lead to an argument that leads to a series of fights that leads to bitterness and resentment and unforgiveness.

Can love cover over all of that? Yes.

We know it can, because God has forgiven us already of all those things, and many other acts and desires and thoughts that we might deem even worse. In His relatively short time walking as a human on this earth, Jesus forgave people for betraying Him, for insulting Him, for giving false testimony about Him, for sinning against His Father, for calling Him crazy, for comparing Him to Satan, for beating Him, and for crucifying Him.

Since God has forgiven us of so much, who are we to refuse to forgive others of so little?

We have to accept that people are human. People will make mistakes. People will make wrong choices. And if we are going to love humans, things are certainly going to get messy. Not just toothpaste-globs-on-the-sink and hairballs-in-the-bathtub kind of messy. But sometimes the words people say will wound us. The things people do will grieve us. And sometimes even the things they don't do will leave a mark on us.

When you love people deeply, you become vulnerable. That doesn't mean you must subject yourself to abusive or toxic relationships. God doesn't tell us that we have to put ourselves in harm's way deliberately so that we can show love to abusers. We have to recognize that some people need to be loved in a way that helps them not to hurt others, to become better than what they are.

But loving others also means you open yourself up to the riches of deep understanding, deep intimacy, deep caring, and deep love. Love covers us when it goes deep enough. And then we learn just a bit more about the love God has for us—the love that is so deep and wide and high and long that it can cover a whole planet full of people.

God, thank You for teaching me how to love deeply. Amen.

Overcoming Unbelief

"I do believe; help me overcome my unbelief!"
MARK 9:24

Does anything trouble a parent more than a son or daughter with a chronic illness? Moms and dads try to endure the stress of such a situation as best as they can. They try to hide their fears and worries from their children. But it's so hard. Day after day, they have to fight for their child's health. They have to deal with health insurance claims and doctor's appointments and medical prescriptions and bills, bills, bills. And sometimes they have to deal with a lot worse—they have to deal with watching their child go through pain.

The father in Mark 9 had caused quite a stir. You can just imagine the lines of desperation on his face. There he is, seeking help from these followers of the Messiah. He's heard about miraculous things—people regaining their sight, paralyzed men walking again, women being restored to good health. But he finally makes it to the potential source of help, and he gets rejected.

Devastation. That must have been what he felt. Where else could he go?

But then Jesus comes. And the Teacher is ready to teach this generation a lesson.

The boy is brought to the Messiah. The father tells again of the sorrow and suffering they have endured together—he and his son. The words must be hard to get out—how many times would he have to tell this story? How many times must he relive all the horrible moments when he thought his son would be killed by the spirit inside him? They had tried to get help from so many places. Not one of us would blame this father for feeling a bit defeated. "If you can do anything, take pity on us and help us," he said (Mark 9:22).

If we took Jesus' next words out of context, they might sound harsh. "'If you can'?" said Jesus. "Everything is possible for one who believes" (verse 23). But Jesus was not mocking the father. He knew how this story was going to end. No, the Rabbi was simply teaching the crowd. It's as if He was saying, "Look, everyone—you could do this if you would really believe in Me. You have access to the power of the living, holy, healing God. You say you believe in this God. But do you?"

Then the father said a prayer that any of us can recognize: "I believe, but I don't think I believe enough. God, help me believe even more!"

And Jesus, in His grace and mercy, showed the man and the whole crowd exactly why they could believe, even more. We can't overcome our unbelief on our own—we need to come to Jesus.

Lord, I do believe in You. Help me believe even more. Amen.

Patterns

*Do not conform to the pattern of this world, but be transformed
by the renewing of your mind. Then you will be able to test and
approve what God's will is— his good, pleasing and perfect will.*

ROMANS 12:2

Frosty snowflake crystals on a cold window. Symmetrical crowns of petals circling yellow flower heads. Geese flying in Vs through a blue autumn sky. Sunrise and sunset, day after day. Waves upon waves crashing onto the shore. Crystal formations deep within the earth.

Nature is filled with beautiful, amazing patterns. We can see evidence of the clever structure and brilliant elegance of God's design everywhere we go.

But often the patterns that people follow are not so pretty. We make mistakes, we hide our mistakes, we lie about our mistakes, we suffer from our mistakes, and we forget them. Then we start that cycle all over again.

We get our feelings hurt, we don't talk about it, we get bitter, we get angry, we get into arguments with people who don't even know what we are talking about. We get hurt again. And we hurt others.

We notice a temptation, we try to control ourselves, we don't talk about it, we get tempted again, we give in, and we hide what we've done. Then it happens all over again.

We say we will do a thing, we get busy, we forget, we do other things, we don't say we are sorry, and then we blame someone else for our neglectful behavior.

Do you recognize any of these cycles? Are these familiar patterns at play in your world, in your town, in your household?

Paul urges us to change things up. Start over. Start new. Be transformed. Be different. How are we supposed to do this? Through the "renewing of your mind." And how does this happen? We're given a clue in the next sentence—we're told that we'll be able to test and approve what God's will is.

Now, how in the world can we test and approve what God's will is if we don't have anything to test it against?

But we do. We have God's Word. We have the testimony of Jesus. We have the wisdom of God poured out to us through others. We have the ability to ask God about it in prayer. By doing these things, by doing what's required to test and approve what God's will is, we can renew our minds. We can get our minds following different thought patterns. We can make ourselves practice different ways of behaving. We can be transformed.

Lord God, change me. Renew my mind. Transform my heart. I want to know Your will. Amen.

More Than Bread

"I am the bread of life. Whoever comes to me will never be hungry again. Whoever believes in me will never be thirsty."
JOHN 6:35 NLT

We ask for patience. God gives us long lines. We ask for courage. God puts us in situations where we have to face our fears. We ask for more power. God shows us how little we are. We ask for safety. God shows us what we have to risk and how much we must depend on Him.

When we ask God for solutions, we shouldn't be surprised when His answers don't look like they go with our questions. God, in His perfect wisdom, gives us exactly what we need when we need it. But He doesn't always give us what we think we want. And that's a good thing.

The huge crowd had been following Jesus for some time, traveling with Him on the dusty roads over rough terrain. They climbed up a hill to sit around the Teacher, and Jesus looked out over the thousands of faces and knew these people were hungry. They didn't have to ask for a lunch break—Jesus knew what they needed. But they didn't just need lunch. They needed to depend on Him.

Later, after Jesus had fed the crowd miraculously with five loaves of bread and two fish, they came looking for Him again. They weren't just hungry for more fish sandwiches. They wanted this power Jesus had. They wanted to be able to perform miracles.

And maybe they wanted to be seen as the kind of people who could perform miracles.

They said they wanted to perform "God's works." And Jesus told them they could. All they had to do was believe in Him.

That was all they had to do. Believe that this Jesus—this man who had just turned bread and fish into a feast right in front of them—was sent from God. Believe that He was who He claimed to be. Believe that He was the way to God, the way to live forever with God in heaven.

But many of them just couldn't do it. No matter what they had seen, they couldn't believe that this fellow from Nazareth, this son of a carpenter, could also be the Son of God. Maybe they weren't ready to believe that God really could do anything. Or maybe they weren't ready to obey this God.

Many of them turned away. They had wanted bread. But Jesus wanted to give them much more than the ability to make a meal for a day. Jesus wanted to feed them for life. And they were missing it. Are we?

Jesus, my Lord and King, help me obey whatever You ask me to do. Amen.

Joy of the Harvest

He said to his disciples, "The harvest is great, but the workers are few. So pray to the Lord who is in charge of the harvest; ask him to send more workers into his fields."
MATTHEW 9:37–38 NLT

Harvesttime in many communities is a time of celebration. In days long past, this was even truer. Farmers had worked hard all spring and summer to plow the land and plant the crops and tend their fields. They might have suffered setbacks and hard times, terrible weather and diseases affecting their plants. But at harvesttime, they could all come together and rejoice in the work they had done. And they could be thankful to God for the results of that work.

At harvesttime, after all the usable parts of the crops are gathered in, the workers finally have a chance to rest. The farmers can take a break from worry and stress and sweat. They reap the rewards of their labor—in money for their crops, in food for their families, but also in the feeling of satisfaction for a job well done.

But other people celebrate at harvesttime too—people who have not toiled in the fields. People who have never worried about hailstorms and freezing temperatures. People who may have never seen the crack of dawn.

A lot of people want to enjoy the benefits of the harvest. They want the food, but they don't want the work. They want the celebration, but they don't want to perform the service.

When Jesus traveled from town to town, He saw so much work that needed to be done. He saw people who were suffering with all kinds of diseases and illnesses. He met people who were hurting in their hearts. And He heard from people who were seeking answers. He saw that so many people were "confused and helpless" (Matthew 9:36 NLT). They didn't know what to do to make their lives better. They didn't know where to go to ask their questions and get good answers. They didn't know who to follow.

Jesus wanted to help them all. He had compassion on them. But even Jesus couldn't be everywhere at once in His human form. And He knew the people would still have needs long after He had left the earth.

But He also knew that people needed to do the work. They needed to come together and serve one another. They needed to feel compassion. They needed to listen to each other's cares and share each other's sorrows. They needed to ask questions together. And then everyone would really know the joy of the harvest.

Lord, send more workers into the fields. Send me, Lord. Amen.

Remember

"Jesus, remember me when you come into your kingdom."
LUKE 23:42

. . . .

We can only imagine what was running through the minds of many people coming back from Calvary after Jesus had been crucified. After all, so many of them had benefited from His powers and so many also from His teaching. He had come to the lost sheep who had been turned out and scorned by the religious authorities. There were folks who wanted to crown Him when He entered Jerusalem! Now He was gone. How had so much promise come to this end?

Yet there was one more conversion in store.

He is the one thief who sees in the final hour that this Jesus was not on the cross on His own behalf; he is the one last person who is drawn to believe that Jesus was not merely of this world, and so he prays to Him, "Jesus, remember me when you come into your kingdom."

George had lost his father almost fifteen years ago, and the one thing that stuck with him was his father's request of his son at the end—that he would not be forgotten. In the first years that his father was gone, George made it a point to visit his grave regularly and take care of things there. Sometimes he would talk to him about life, hoping that somehow his father would hear him. But as more time went on, he lost the spirit in which he had been doing that, and the memory of his father just became more and more tenuous. But one Lenten season, when George heard the words of the thief on the cross, they lit a spark in his heart, and he began to pray to Jesus too.

Instead of standing on his own in trying to keep his father alive in this world, he enlisted the truest help he knew, the help of Jesus. And so he prayed like the thief and asked to remember his father. He asked Jesus to remember him too, and to bring him and his father together one day in His kingdom. He realized that all of those people who must have been dismayed and disappointed at the crucifixion did not have the hope of the thief, did not have the hope of so many people today who know that Jesus has been raised from the dead.

George only wished now that he'd had this realization on the day his father had died. Then they could have prayed together to Jesus. But that thought inspired him to head back out to the cemetery and speak to his father as in years past. "Come on, Dad; let's pray together. 'Jesus, remember me when you come into your kingdom.'"

Jesus, remember me too. Amen.

Where Your Heart Is

"For where your treasure is,
there your heart will be also."
Matthew 6:21

One thing we can ask ourselves about our spiritual lives is exactly what our intentions and goals are in making the appearances that we make and doing the things that we do. Are we proud that we attend services each weekend, making the effort to attend them? Do we boast about it, if only to ourselves? What is there to boast about? Among our friends, is our attendance a badge of honor? What exactly is the honor?

Granted, in a world abounding with scoffers, the temptation is great to boast, and to throw our faith and our spiritual constancy in the faces of those who taunt us. But then we might ask ourselves, *For whom am I attending when I am present at services? Toward whom is my focus directed? Am I locked into some earthly battle with earthly adversaries over whom I wish to triumph? About whose praises am I finally concerned, those of the people around me or those of God? And who is it, exactly, that I am worshipping? Is it God, or is it me?*

Sal and Alex are two neighborly friends. Alex gets up every day, rain or shine, to get himself to the gym. According to him, his routine is directed at his health more than his "six-pack," although he talks more about his six-pack than his health.

Sal, on the other hand, gets to the gym two or three times a week. But every morning of just about every day, Sal makes it his business to sit on the back porch or stretch out on the couch with his Bible or his prayer book. He spends forty-five minutes to an hour each morning sustaining and strengthening his relationship with Jesus. He gleans whatever wisdom he can from his reading, and he has a running dialogue with his Lord and Master. He talks to Him about his cares and his worries. He prays for his children and his siblings, and for all the people who have no one to pray for them.

Regularly enough, Alex asks Sal to come to the gym with him, and from time to time, Sal accepts the invitation. He always enjoys the physical activity and the camaraderie. But in the end, he asks himself about his limited time and how he should spend it. Should he be worrying about getting fit, or should he be working harder to serve God well? Sal often finds himself thinking that only God knows how we appear; only God knows about our true treasure and where it is that we are trying to store it up.

Lord, help me to make sure that where I'm spending
my time and treasure is where You are. Amen.

That Kind of Peace

And the peace of God, which transcends all understanding,
will guard your hearts and your minds in Christ Jesus.
PHILIPPIANS 4:7

When a very best friend is sitting with you, everything looks a little better. Even when sad or frustrating things might have brought you together for a time, the comfort of having someone who knows you well close by to care for you is the best feeling in the world. It doesn't really matter what gets said or done; just a squeeze of the hand is a kind of sweet medicine, soothing your soul and giving you strength.

Paul tells us that "the Lord is near" (Philippians 4:5). Now, for some, that statement could produce fear. For if the Lord is near, then He is close enough to see what we are doing and to hear what we are saying. And why is He so near? Is He here to deliver punishments to us? No, not in this case. The Lord is near because He is always near in this way. He always comes close to those He loves, and who love Him.

And with this perfect Best Friend beside us, we know for sure that we don't have to be afraid of anything. We don't have to be worried. We don't have to stress about how to solve a problem. Through prayer and petition, and with thanks, we can present our requests to Him, and He will answer us. Because that's what best friends do. They come when you need help. No matter how far away they are, they offer real, tangible help in some way.

And that's how the peace that is deeper than any other kind of peace arrives. God's peace pours over us, filling us and surrounding us like a gushing stream. Even when the world looks bleak, when we can't see an answer, when we are burdened with stress and worries, God's peace can push through all of that and fill up our hearts—untangling the knots in our minds and soothing our spirits. It's the kind of sure footing we feel when we make a decision that puts us in line with His will. It's the supernatural calm we are able to cling to when storms are roaring all around us. It's the quiet confidence that allows us to step into situations that would otherwise shake us. It's the peace that we don't understand, that we can't describe, and that doesn't make sense. It's that kind of peace.

Lord, I'm so thankful You are near me when troubles come.
Bless me with Your impossible peace. Amen.

Faith Together

But let each one take heed how he builds on [the foundation].
1 CORINTHIANS 3:10 NKJV

Why do we have divisions among us? Why do we quarrel with each other?

Pride. When we let our pride be our focus, we lose sight of loving and caring for one another. Pride causes us to feel that it's important to be acknowledged. It's important to have our contributions recognized. It's necessary to be known.

But why? Maybe because we feel that unless we grab attention, no one will give it to us. Unless we announce ourselves, no one will remember us. Maybe we are afraid that God will not consider us valuable.

Paul talked about divisions within the body of believers. He said some were claiming to be followers of one leader over another, as if who they followed—other than Jesus—gave them some kind of superior status. But he pointed out how silly this was. For one person might have planted the seed of faith, and another might have nurtured that faith in the church, but all of the growing and believing and learning could have come only through the grace of God. The miracle of people coming to Christ and surrendering their lives to Him comes only through the grace of God. The ability to understand His Word and hear His Spirit comes only through the grace of God.

And God, of course, values us. He paid the ultimate price for each one of us, and He calls us to do His work. He would not do any of that unless He thought we were worth it.

The work we do for His kingdom is of special interest to Him. It is our duty to represent Him well, so we must build on the foundation of faith with work that is good and true and sound. Then when it is tested by the troubles that come, the wisdom and truth and goodness of our work will stand. But this kind of building work isn't easy. It is, however, all too easy for us to let pride cloud our judgment.

That's why it's important for us to work together. None of us should try to lead others on our own. None of us should try to teach based on our knowledge only. We need to work together so that no one person becomes too arrogant and so that people don't become too dependent on one human being. We also need to work together so we can learn from each other and counsel each other and offer grace to each other when we make mistakes. And we need to work together with God. We need to cover every project—especially missions of outreach to those who don't yet know God—with prayer, asking God for help and listening to His guidance through His Word and through the Spirit.

Lord, I know I'd be nowhere without You. Help me to give You all the glory. Amen.

Ruled by Christ

For in Christ all the fullness of the Deity lives in bodily form,
and in Christ you have been brought to fullness.
COLOSSIANS 2:9–10

Rules. We really like them, don't we? At least when they are on our side. We like having a framework of fairness. We like being able to tell when someone is stepping outside the lines. We like to have standards to reach and targets to shoot for.

But sometimes the rules we humans make can actually rule us. For every time we are told not to step on the grass, there will arise some situation in which the grass must be stepped on. For every speed limit, there will be some emergency when speeding is necessary. For every time a door says "Do Not Enter," we can think of a scenario in which it would be impossible not to go through that door.

Does that mean rules are made to be broken? No. It just means rules are made by humans. And they are made *for* humans, to help us. If the rules are not helping, then they need to be reevaluated.

The Colossians were having trouble with some rules. Some people were telling them they couldn't be Christians unless they did certain things and followed certain rules. But entry into the kingdom of God is not controlled by human rules. On the contrary, all you need to be a Christian is Christ.

When Christ came to earth, He came as a human—fully God in a fully human form. He came that way on purpose—to be near us, but also to show us that it is possible to follow God as a human, living in a human body, bound by human limitations. He came to us as a full human to show us how to become fully what God designed us to be. Belonging to Christ is not based on human traditions or laws written by human hands. When we give our lives to Christ, and are buried in baptism, we are raised in Him through faith alone—not through any acts we perform. We die to our old lives and God makes us alive in Christ. It is that simple. And it is that mysterious.

Having wise rules as guides for living is a good thing. But we should never think either that we can gain the fullness of Christ through following earthly rules or that we can somehow lose the life we have in Christ through breaking those rules. All we need is Christ.

Jesus, thank You for making the way to You so
easy to see. Help me not to lose sight of it. Amen.

Gentle Power

He gathers the lambs in his arms
and carries them close to his heart.
Isaiah 40:11

He had a leathery face, aged by the elements much more than by his years. A somewhat unkempt beard gave him an impression of gruffness, and he generally wore old, tattered clothing when he was out in the fields. In the world of those who are in the position of taking care of little lambs, this shepherd was about as far away as you could imagine from "Mary" of nursery song fame.

But when he gathered up little lambs in his arms, he was gentle and tender as could be. He would smooth down the little lambs' big ears and speak softly to them, warning them to stay close to the flock and not stray too far. Then he would set them back down among the herd and go on his way, but he always kept an eye out for the helpless, silly little lambs.

Our God is like that shepherd—strong and enduring, patient and ever watchful. How reassuring to know that the King of the universe has His eye on us! He will not stop us from stumbling now and then—He knows that we learn great lessons through the mistakes we make. But He will not let us be attacked with no defense.

The God who "measured the waters in the hollow of his hand, or with the breadth of his hand marked off the heavens" (Isaiah 40:12) is the same God who puts no limits on His love for us. The God who "held the dust of the earth in a basket, or weighed the mountains on the scales and the hills in a balance" (verse 12) is the same God who wisely judges our thoughts and actions, and yet offers us infinite mercy. The God whose Spirit is unfathomable and whose mind is boundless generously shares with us His wisdom. He understands us better than we understand ourselves, and He offers us perfect counsel for every situation.

The God who "sits enthroned above the circle of the earth" (verse 22) is the One who bows low to serve us. The God who "stretches out the heavens like a canopy" (verse 22) is the One who reaches across the darkness to welcome us into His beautiful light.

The God who has "great power and mighty strength" (verse 26) does not let any one of us go missing—He knows us each by name and calls us to Him. Like a strong shepherd, our God scoops us up when we are far away from Him and holds us tightly to His heart. He whispers to us to stay close and not stray too far. And then He lets us go again.

Lord, I love Your gentle power. Please protect me. Amen.

Stop Judging

"Do not judge, or you too will be judged. For in the same way you judge others, you will be judged, and with the measure you use, it will be measured to you."
MATTHEW 7:1–2

Without question, in living out our lives, we are all charged with judging. A parent looking out for children has to know what is safe and what is not, what is a healthy activity and what is not, who is suitable as a companion and who is not. And in various aspects of our lives, we are called upon in like manner to judge.

Jesus surely knew this fact, so what exactly is He driving at when He instructs us to "stop judging"? The way that He puts His teaching suggests that whenever we find ourselves judging another, we should make sure we put ourselves in the shoes of the person we are judging and ask ourselves this: Am I willing to be held up to the same scrutiny and judgment? If I must judge, am I using a standard that I would be willing to have used in my own case?

Rosemary's friend Claire told her that she and her husband were going through a rough patch in their marriage. Claire's husband was a bit heavy-handed with the children, although not so much with her. But when she tried to help him with parenting, he grew resentful about her advice and angry with her. Rosemary found herself feeling pretty angry and disappointed with Aaron, Claire's husband. So Rosemary was deliberately distant and chilly with Aaron whenever he was around. She decided he just wasn't a likable person.

Claire didn't realize how judgmental Rosemary would be about the situation. She couldn't find the words to explain it, but Rosemary's cold treatment of her husband wasn't helpful to Claire at all. On the contrary, it made things more difficult, because now Claire felt she had to arrange to see Rosemary only when Aaron wasn't around.

When Claire finally decided to tell Aaron how she had been feeling, she didn't tell Rosemary right away. However, her conversation with her husband went remarkably well. He really took her words to heart. Aaron told Claire that he'd been thinking about her advice for dealing with the boys and would try to do better. Claire couldn't have been happier, but she wondered what Rosemary would think. The next time she saw her friend, she told her what had transpired. Rosemary blushed and said, "I guess I was a little quick on the judgment trigger. Next time I'll remember that 'mercy triumphs over judgment'" (James 2:13).

Lord, it's so easy for me to rush to judgment, especially when I think I know who's right and who's wrong. Help me to be quicker to offer mercy. Amen.

Forgiven Much

*"She was forgiven many, many sins, and so she is very, very grateful.
If the forgiveness is minimal, the gratitude is minimal."*
Luke 7:47 MSG

Jerry stood outside the door to his father's home office. His brother Steve was in the office with their father in trouble again. Steve was attracted to trouble like flies to overripe fruit. You name it, Steve had done it: petty vandalism, shoplifting, public drunkenness and disorderly behavior. After a while, it seemed like the whole family was on hold, waiting for the next time a call came in from the local police station wanting someone to come vouch for Steve.

Their parents were always terrified of what would happen to him, so they routinely bailed him out of his difficulties. Jerry had felt sorry for Steve for a long while, but then he began to feel exasperated and embarrassed to be forever defending his antics. Jerry's friends went from thinking Steve was cool to thinking he was a loser. Finally, Jerry concluded that his friends were right; his brother was a loser, plain and simple.

Recently, Steve had been caught at school in possession of drugs—not a lot, but enough to get him suspended for a few days. Steve was talking to their father about what he was going to do to get himself straightened out. While Steve seemed to be really shaken this time, being suspended and all, Jerry found it hard to believe him, never mind forgive him.

Later, when Steve emerged from the office, Jerry made it his business to talk to his father. "Why do you keep putting up with him?"

His father looked at him then looked away. "Well," he said finally, "it's not always for the same reason. First I thought it was just youthful mistakes, but after a while that changed. Then he seemed to me to be just a young man with a devil-may-care attitude, out for a good time. I don't know. But now, Steve seems to be genuinely concerned about himself; maybe it was something that somebody said to him at school, I can't say. But he seems sincerely sorry; and yes, one more time, we're going to forgive him. He actually said that he was sorry because he knows how much we love him, and he said he's going to change because he loves us. What do you think of that, Jerry?"

Jerry stared at his father for a few seconds then shrugged his shoulders. "I don't know, Dad. I love you too. I hope that counts for something."

*Lord, help me to understand when things don't
seem fair. Thank You for forgiving me. Amen.*

Glorious Sight

"Rabbi, I want to see."
MARK 10:51

Many of us have experienced the wonder of some beautiful sight. It could be something as commonplace as a beautiful sunrise or sunset, a dogwood or a rosebush in full bloom. At those times, we find ourselves treasuring the world around us and spontaneously rendering praise to God for the gift of His creation. But most days there is none of that. We merely walk through the world apathetic and unseeing. We walk through the world as if there were something inconsequential or insignificant about the things we observe. At those times, we are blind to the world, and our power of sight is unavailing to us. We not only fail to see the beauty around us; we fail to see what a gift God has granted to us in the very power of sight, our way into the corridors of God's splendor.

There is hardly need to speculate about Bartimaeus, the blind man in Mark's Gospel, and the visual experience of the world that he had after Jesus healed him. How glorious the colors must have seemed to him! How bright! How deep! How rich! The passage tells us that after he gained his sight, he followed Jesus. How grateful he must have been to Jesus, who through His power had revealed the glory of God's creation to him.

We are not completely unlike Bartimaeus. We too want to see. But what do we want to see? Is it just another curio, another bauble, another chestnut for our catalog of lovely things? Or do we want to see the world that the cured blind man saw? Do we want to see the world God has given to us in all its splendor, not worn down and exhausted and drained by overfamiliarity, overexposure, and careless attention, but fresh and vibrant and burgeoning with vitality.

We are unlike the blind man in one crucial way. Most of us have never been blind; we have never had to struggle in that way, and so we take for granted our sight and the sights. In Mark's passage, Jesus has pity on the blind man. He asks him what he wants Jesus to do for him. "Master, I want to see," comes his plea.

Jesus is asking each of us too, "What do you want Me to do for you?" We might answer, "Master, I want to see the world that Bartimaeus the blind man saw. I too want to see a world so full of God's glory that all I want to do is follow Him."

Lord, grant me the ability to see and appreciate
all the beauty You have created for us. Amen.

Calm

Muscles taut, mouth open, lips curled, teeth bared, eyes wide, brow furrowed, fists clenched, body leaning forward—it takes a lot of physical energy to throw oneself into a rage. It takes a lot of mental and emotional energy as well. When we let anger overtake us, we are pushed to throw everything out of us and at another person—we want to unload the anger, the irritation, the hatred. All the bad feelings come rushing out of us at once in the form of careless words and uncontrolled actions.

Sometimes these explosions happen because we've allowed negative feelings to build up too long over time. We let small offenses wound us and then, instead of caring for those wounds and asking God to heal them, we pick at those hurts until they are infected with anger and resentment. This infection spreads through us, so that the next time someone insults us or neglects us, we add on that pain as well. We carry around this tumor of stored-up annoyance until it becomes far weightier than any one of those issues should have been. In fact, our tangle of emotions and memories and hurtful thoughts becomes too much for us to manage.

Instead of dealing with it, instead of talking about our feelings with someone we trust and doing something healthy with the energy of our emotions, we let our feelings change us. We let our feelings affect our relationships. We sometimes let our feelings rule our lives.

But after an outburst, what happens? Usually calm comes. When that energy is let out, we realize how tiring it has been to carry it, and we rest. The problem is, if we have released our anger in such a way that it hurts others, we now have a new pain to deal with.

The wise person can avoid this kind of trouble. When we get irritated, we can talk about it with someone who knows us and who can help us find a beneficial way to deal with that irritation. Some offenses are small and need to be overlooked and put away. But some will need more attention. We may need to talk to the offender. We may need to ask God to help us forgive. We may need to seek more counsel. We may just need time.

When we deal with the sources of our anger intentionally and carefully, we can bring calm to our lives without hurting anyone. We can bring calm that comes from being content with ourselves and with others, knowing that we have access to the peace of God.

*Lord, help me not to be foolish. Help me to
be wise in dealing with my anger. Amen.*

Overflowing

May the God of hope fill you with all joy and peace as you trust in him,
so that you may overflow with hope by the power of the Holy Spirit.
ROMANS 15:13

Toward the end of his letter to the Romans, Paul blesses his audience. He entreats the Lord to allow their faith in Him and in the Church to be accompanied by "joy and peace." What does it mean to have faith in the Lord that brings us joy and peace? What does it mean to be a person filled with hope through the Spirit?

Tom is the father of three children, two boys sandwiching a girl. His children were the apples of his eye when they were growing up, and now they are grown with children of their own. Tom was always a man of solid faith, and he raised the children in the faith, building the churchgoing habit into each one. On top of that, he made it his business to get them out into the different parts of the country so that they could see and experience natural beauty. They traveled to the forests of northern New England, rich with thick foliage. They sat on the beaches along the east coast. They went out west to witness the stunning beauty of the mountains and the canyons and the huge expanses of sky. They visited the forests of California to see ancient trees and to gaze on the very different waters of the Pacific.

Wherever he took them, Tom made it a point to open their eyes and minds and hearts to their belief that this creation is God's gift to us human beings. He encouraged them to consider that all these wondrous things were examples on top of examples of God's love for us. And he taught them that human beings are no less wondrous than any of these other beauties, and that God has supplied them with the gift of faith just so they can understand and grasp the other things He has given them.

Now, when Tom saw his children with their children, teaching them how to pray and reading Bible stories to them, he often found himself smiling with joy in his heart for his own gift of faith. And when he reflected on his faith community and the many people who joined him and his wife in teaching their children, he often felt filled by the Spirit with hope that the chaos and noise of the world will give way to the beauty and order promised by Jesus' resurrection.

Lord, I know no hope I have comes from me. Thank You for
the faith that lets me see beyond all my troubles. Amen.

Give Your Widow's Mite

*"Truly I tell you," he said, "this poor widow
has put in more than all the others."*
LUKE 21:3

. . . .

The story of the widow's offering presents a unique challenge to each of us. At first blush, it seems to diminish those who give from their surplus—after all, they can afford it. But further reflection uncovers a deeper meaning that Jesus had in mind with His observation. Jesus wants us to consider our worldly situations and ask ourselves just what it is that God may want from us.

Caleb operates a modest-size farm in northeastern Ohio, and he makes a good living for a farmer. He lives with his wife, Barb, and their two children, a boy and a girl. They live an active life, of course, but beyond the demands of the farm, a quiet life. They spend regular family time together, and they attend church services every Sunday, barring any event out of the ordinary.

Caleb gets the most enjoyment out of farming tomatoes. He loves the fruit itself for sure, but the thing he really loves is growing high-quality tomatoes, getting them just right for fresh-air markets and good eating. Caleb has a regular stand at a few markets within reasonable distance, and the compliments he lives for are those about his tomatoes.

Among the tomatoes that Caleb grows, his prize ones are heirloom tomatoes. Caleb has always devoted a portion of his field to those, and Barb often jokes that he dotes on those tomatoes more than he dotes on the children. But the peculiar thing is that Caleb sells only a small portion of the heirlooms, for which he gets the best price, and the rest he donates to food pantries for the hungry. At Thanksgiving and Christmas, he is ready with these gems upon request. While he is quite pleased to do this, everyone around him wonders about it.

One day when he was dropping off a donation, his friend Curtis took him aside and said, "You know, Caleb, you've got a lot of tomatoes out on that farm of yours. You could donate plenty of those; you don't have to bring in these specialties."

"No, no, no," Caleb chuckled. Then, leaning toward Curtis as if to tell him a secret, Caleb said, "This is my 'widow's mite.' You're right, I've got plenty, but they're not nearly as good as these beauties. So I take pleasure in giving the heirlooms away. Now what do you think the good Lord thinks of that?"

Curtis shook his head and laughed. "Widow's mite," he repeated. "I think the good Lord is probably smiling, that's what."

Lord, help me give the best of me to You. Amen.

Stumbling

To him who is able to keep you from stumbling and to present
you before his glorious presence without fault and with great joy—
to the only God our Savior be glory, majesty, power and authority,
through Jesus Christ our Lord, before all ages, now and forevermore! Amen.
JUDE 24–25

A stubbed toe. Dropped papers. Spilled coffee. These are all likely results of stumbling. Usually, stumbling does not result in any horrible, life-changing consequences.

But it all depends on where you stumble, doesn't it?

Stumbling up a flight of steps might leave you with a bruised shin or two. Stumbling down a flight of steps might give you a broken neck.

Stumbling along an uneven sidewalk might result in a bruised ego—especially if people are watching. Stumbling along an uneven path on the side of a mountain could lead to your death.

The stumbling Jude was referring to when he wrote to believers was a serious matter with serious consequences. It was a spiritual stumbling, the kind that could lead a person to fall into eternal fire. The examples he gives as reminders are of those who were destroyed for their lack of faith, of angels who rejected their places and are now bound in darkness, and of those who succumbed to immorality and perversion and now suffer punishment forever.

People who stumble in this way, and who keep walking on bumpy roads on purpose, are those Jude describes as "clouds without rain, blown along by the wind; autumn trees, without fruit and uprooted—twice dead. They are wild waves of the sea, foaming up their shame; wandering stars, for whom blackest darkness has been reserved forever" (verses 12–13). In other words, they are people who seem at first as if they have something to offer—people who may appear to be friendly, or wise, or charming, or good—but then turn out to care only about themselves and their desires.

We've probably all met people like this—perhaps we've even been hurt by them. But there is a way to protect ourselves from getting entangled with toxic men and women who try to make us fall. We can build ourselves up in our faith by reading God's Word and listening to Him every day. We can pray in the Holy Spirit. We can love others and learn to love them well, following the example of Jesus. We can be aware of and express gratitude for the mercy of God and offer mercy to others who are in danger of stumbling too—extending a hand to help them find their balance again.

God my Savior and King, I'm so thankful not only that You are able
to keep me from stumbling, but that You are willing to do so. Amen.

Open Hearts

*"That's true, Lord, but even dogs are allowed to
eat the scraps that fall beneath their masters' table."*
MATTHEW 15:27 NLT

The Lord God sees all of His children. At any moment He can open hearts to reach out to Him and receive Him. So it is that we have this Canaanite woman crying out to Jesus to rid her daughter of the demon haunting her soul. Jesus first remains silent, then informs her of His specific mission to the house of Israel. The disciples want to drive her away, but she remains undaunted. She has been graced with complete faith in this Jesus, complete faith that He is the Lord whom she believes Him to be, and she gives herself over to that faith. Even knowing her status, as someone who is not a Jew approaching this honored Rabbi, she asks the Lord to remember that even dogs eat the scraps of their masters' feasts.

Her remark to Jesus appears to indicate the breadth of her faith and her insight. God goes far beyond human outsiders in providing for His creation. Even dogs get sustenance. God in His goodness and love has opened up her heart, Gentile woman though she is. Suddenly through the plenitude of God's love, the mission has expanded. And Jesus, Lord that He is, meets the faith-filled Canaanite woman and rewards that faith.

The Lord God today continues to open hearts to receive Him. The Spirit continues to fortify those whose hearts are open with the strength to persevere in prayer, in calling out to the Lord for the help and guidance they need.

Michelle was one of those people. Her parents were fallen-away Christians, and she had not been baptized. But when she began to read parts of the Bible, Michelle found herself awakening to the reality that God was opening her heart to His voice. At her college, several students belonged to a Christian campus group. The group had a common meal together on Thursday evenings and she accepted an invitation to the supper. At first she found herself drawn to the group by the friendliness and thoughtfulness of the members, but she became fully attracted to the study and the prayer in which they engaged. In the course of time, she engaged an older member to be a sort of mentor who could help her learn about the Christian faith and answer the questions she might have. If the Lord God was showing Himself to her, she wanted to answer His call. "Have mercy on me, oh Lord," she prayed one night, giving her heart to Christ. She felt such contentment after her acceptance of Jesus, almost as if she had eaten a delicious feast.

Lord Jesus, open my heart to You more and more every day. Amen.

Letting Go

When Jesus heard this, he said to him, "You still lack one thing. Sell everything you have and give to the poor, and you will have treasure in heaven. Then come, follow me."
LUKE 18:22

. . . .

We human beings are strongly attached to our material possessions, and so it was with the rich man in Luke 18 whom Jesus told to sell all his things: "When he heard this, he became very sad, because he was very wealthy" (verse 23). Indeed, Jesus' disciples are themselves flabbergasted by His comment about the difficulty the rich face in attaining the "kingdom of God"—that it's harder than passing a camel through a needle's eye. They ask, If the rich can't get into heaven, then who can? They still think that the worldly rich must enjoy God's favor. Jesus clearly thinks otherwise.

Oliver was a man of considerable gifts. By the time of his early middle age, he had amassed a considerable amount of wealth. Money was no obstacle between him and his desires. His success also secured other advantages for him. He had a beautiful wife and two daughters; he had rich friends, and he enjoyed the respect and adoration of many people.

Oliver went to church on Sundays because it was a thing to do. Yet he didn't feel much like he needed church. He donated money regularly, often joking to others that that was why the pastor wanted him there. But in truth, he looked down on faith, feeling it was a crutch that some people, even many people, needed. But he did not. Oliver thought that all the credit for his success belonged to him. There were no miracles involved and never any experience that would make him think that God had anything to do with it. In his world, he was completely self-sufficient; really, he was God.

One Monday when he was reflecting on his outlook on life, he recalled hearing about the rich man. A little voice in his head prodded him, "You're not God, not even close. You're going to die one day and be forgotten in a short space of time. If you want to be holy like God is holy, then give it all away." When he woke from his reverie, he realized that his fortune was *his* crutch and he would be terrified without it. He didn't give his riches away, but he did begin to see how hard it was for him to be closer to God. And he began from that day to pray earnestly for spiritual courage.

*Lord, sometimes my troubles come not from what I don't have,
but from what I refuse to give up. Help me hold on to You instead. Amen.*

Just Pray

Is anyone among you in trouble? Let them pray.
Is anyone happy? Let them sing songs of praise.
James 5:13

. . . .

The first step you need to take when you find yourself feeling troubled by what's happening directly to you or what's going on around you is pretty simple.

Pray.

Now here's the funny thing. You're not going to want to do it. On your best days, you think you will. You think, of course, that when trouble comes, you'll pray. That makes all kinds of sense. Of course God wants us to bring Him our burdens. Of course we need to tell our heavenly Father what's going on. Of course.

But friend, you are not going to want to pray. You are going to want to fret. You are going to want to complain to someone. You are going to want to compare notes. You are going to want to take charge. You are going to want to take over. You are going to want to run away. You are going to want someone else to do it. You are going to want to hide under the covers. You are going to want to procrastinate. You are going to want to go to a movie. You are going to want to distract yourself. You are going to want to cry. You are going to want to get angry with somebody. You are going to want to eat chocolate.

You are not going to want to settle down and pray.

Why?

There could be all kinds of reasons. But the two that pop up most often are these: (1) You don't think you're good enough. (2) You doubt that God is good enough.

You know that "the prayer of a righteous person is powerful and effective" (James 5:16). But what about the prayer of a sometimes-righteous person? What about a pretty good person? What about a wannabe-righteous person? It's hard to imagine that your prayers will be all that powerful and effective. But what if they were?

You know the Lord can make the sick person well. You know God can offer forgiveness. In theory. But when it comes right down to it, you wonder—will God really bring about good in this situation? Or, perhaps, is God's idea of good here the same as ours?

And the answer to that last question is no. God's idea of good is much better than we can ever imagine. He is vastly more gracious than we have the capacity to be. He is more merciful. He is more generous. He is more faithful.

So go ahead. Are you in trouble? Pray. Are you happy? Pray and give thanks. Are you sick? Pray and ask for healing. Just pray, pray, pray.

Lord, hear my prayer. Amen.

Transformations

His mother said to the servants,
"Whatever He says to you, do it."
JOHN 2:5 NKJV

. . . .

In the scene from the wedding feast at Cana, we can hardly help wondering about the relationship between Jesus and His mother, Mary. How did Jesus relate to Mary as a mother? What did Mary know and understand about Jesus, her Son? On His part, Jesus appears to be taken aback by His mother's declaration that the wine had run short. He immediately takes her statement as a request. In answering, Jesus dismisses his mother's observation, asking, "What does your concern have to do with Me?" (John 2:4 NKJV). He seems to be thinking solely of His own situation: "My hour has not yet come" (verse 4 NKJV). In responding that way, Jesus apparently takes for granted that Mary understands what He is saying.

We can wonder, What for Jesus would mark the fact that His time had indeed come? Did He have that clearly in His mind and heart? From Mary, we get some understanding of Jesus and what He can do. We also see in Mary great confidence that Jesus *will* do something to help, as she instructs the servants, "Whatever He says to you, do it." At the same time, the generality of her command (*whatever* He tells you) seems to indicate that she has little or no idea what Jesus will say or do.

Out of this mysterious exchange comes a miracle—Jesus' first miracle according to John's account. The miracle strongly suggests that the new way, the Way that is Jesus, will not be completely coordinated with the old way. Jesus asks the servers to fill to the brim the very large vessels used for the ritual washings. Jesus seems to have no concern about the purification rites.

The wedding feast at Cana turns out to be the stepping-out occasion for Jesus. The important line in the story appears to come from the mouth of Mary, Jesus' mother. She tells the servants, "Whatever He says to you, do it." The servants were right there to hear Jesus' instructions, but we, we have to be on the lookout for His orders. We may also wonder that even if we believe we hear something, then what next? In the story there is a transformation: the water becomes wine, and it becomes very good wine. And that seems to hold a promise for us too. If we listen and heed, there will be a transformation in each of us, in the people around us whom we affect, and in our world.

♥ · ♥ · · ♥ · ·

Lord, use me as You will, to do what You will,
for the good of Your will. Amen.

Closing the Gap

"There is a great chasm separating us."
LUKE 16:26 NLT

In Luke's story about Lazarus the beggar and the purple-robed rich man, it is not until the death of the rich man and his request of "Father Abraham" to have Lazarus quench his thirst that we hear about the "great chasm" that prevents such a movement. But when we reflect on the story, we see that the great chasm that exists in the afterlife is a reflection of another chasm, the chasm that existed between the rich man and Lazarus in their lives in this world. It is the chasm that exists between the rich and the poor.

The difference between the two chasms, as one can see plainly, is that nothing is preventing the rich man from reaching out to Lazarus begging at his door—nothing, that is, except the blind eye that he continually turns toward the beggar.

Tim and Laura live in a comfortable community outside the city. They send their two children to the school in their neighborhood. While there is not the slightest evidence of poverty or homelessness in their community, Tim is acquainted with the fact of poverty because he works in the city. On his way to work and, in fact, right around his office building, he sees quite a few people begging for food and water and squatting in doorways and alleyways for shelter. Tim gives when he has some loose dollars in his wallet, and when he doesn't, he feels guilty and a little ashamed to boot.

"Here I am," he complained to Laura one evening, "going to church every Sunday, listening to the Word, and I walk by this utter poverty on a daily basis. I feel so helpless." But after hearing the minister preach on the story of Lazarus, Tim took the lesson to heart. He began talking with colleagues in his building and then made up a flyer that he posted and distributed to bring together an area coalition at a local restaurant.

At the meeting, Tim proposed that they undertake to address the poverty and homelessness haunting their business district. "I don't want to chase away these people; I'm proposing that we try to identify them, by name, and then work with them to get them to something closer to stability. If we make a concerted effort," he told his business colleagues and neighbors, "we can at least change the perception of who these people are; that they're not dangerous, just homeless and in need of basics." Tim closed with the idea that had come to him earlier in the day. "We can call our initiative Closing the Gap."

Lord, I can't solve every problem on my own,
but help me do what I can with what I have. Amen.

JOURNAL YOUR WAY TO A DEEPER FAITH

The 5-Minute Prayer Plan Journal for Women

Many Christians yearn for a dynamic prayer life, but we often get stuck in a repetitive routine of prayer. This practical and inspirational journal will give you new ways to approach prayer with 90 focused 5-minute plans for your daily quiet time. These prayer plans explore a variety of life themes appropriate for women of all ages.

Spiral Bound / 978-1-64352-506-8 / $9.99

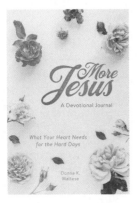

More Jesus: A Devotional Journal

More than 100 devotional readings and prayers fill this journal—touching on topics like illness, anxiety, loss, failure, and worry—will breathe fresh hope and peace into your spirit on the difficult days and every day in between.

Flexible Casebound / 978-1-64352-899-1 / $12.99